A Survival Guide for

Culinary Professionals

by ~~Alan Gelb and Karen Levine~~

THOMSON

DELMAR LEARNING

Australia Canada Mexico ... ngdom United States

THOMSON

DELMAR LEARNING

A Survival Guide for Culinary Professionals
Alan Gelb and Karen Levine

Vice President, Career Education Strategic Business Unit:
Dawn Gerrain

Director of Editorial:
Sherry Gomoll

Acquisitions Editor:
Matthew Hart

Editorial Assistant:
Lisa Flatley

Director of Production:
Wendy A. Troeger

Production Manager:
Carolyn Miller

Production Editor:
Kathryn B. Kucharek

Director of Marketing:
Wendy Mapstone

Cover Design:
Joe Villanova

Library of Congress
Cataloging-in-Publication Data

Gelb, Alan.
  A survival guide for culinary professionals / Alan Gelb and Karen Levine.
    p. cm.
  Includes index.
  ISBN 1-4018-4092-2
1. Food service. 2. Cookery.   I. Levine, Karen. II. Title.
  TX911.G4297 2005
  647.95'023–dc22

2004046053

Contents

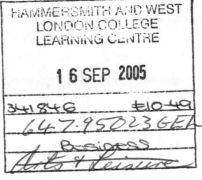

Acknowledgments

We would like to thank the many professionals who took the time to share their thoughts, insights, and reflections. We would particularly like to thank Anthony J. (Toby) Strianese, Chairperson of Hotel, Culinary Arts and Tourism Department, Schenectady County Community College, for all of his expertise and advice. We would also like to thank Lisa Flatley of Thomson Delmar Learning for her help.

Chapter 1

The Right Ingredients

*A*s a culinary professional—whether you're a chef, cook, caterer, or member of the kitchen brigade—you experience your world, and perhaps even the world at large, in a distinct way. Your work requires you to be sensitive to issues around food—taste, balance, the need for organization, and the understanding that many hands stir the pot—and your awareness of how these issues work in the kitchen may very well affect the way you go about living your life in general. On the other hand, you may sometimes be weighed down by the feeling that you have bitten off more than you can chew. You knew the restaurant business was going to be hard . . . but does it have to be *this* hard?

1

So how are you feeling about this field you've chosen for yourself? How is the reality shaping up against the dream? Are you more exhausted than energized? Do you feel yourself hating your customers half the time? Do you work in a kitchen where there is a real team spirit, or are you laboring under some lunatic who doesn't even know how to season his or her soup? Are you where you wanted to be when you set out? Do you have a five-year plan? A 10-year plan? Do you dare dream about opening your own restaurant? Do you enjoy wonderful daydreams about preparing *tapas* for Hollywood stars, or do you suffer nightmares about somebody cracking a tooth on an olive pit you somehow let slip by?

One thing is for sure: making your way in the restaurant world is no piece of cake. (But it does lend itself to plenty of puns!) Seriously, though, it *is* a hard business. To say that it is anything else would mean telling less than the truth. But it also can be a wonderful life.

For starters, people who have trained and developed their culinary skills can expect to enjoy an excellent income. There are more jobs out there for people who possess these skills than there are people to fill them, and that represents a real head start in a tough world. But most people who choose to go into the culinary field do not do so simply because they expect to make a good living, or so that they can have benefits, or because one day they'll enjoy the fruits of a good pension. There are easier ways to ensure such things, if that's what you're basically looking for. People go into this world because they love food, the way some people go into teaching because they love children, or into veterinary science because they love animals, or into aviation because they love the wild blue yonder. And why shouldn't they? Most people in this world would love food if they had enough good experiences with it.

Food, after all, *is* worthy of love. It's what keeps us alive, brings back sweet memories, makes a dreary day more palatable, and comforts us in times of distress. After September 11, 2001, many restaurants rushed to put meat loaf and mashed potatoes and rice pudding on their menus, for nothing seemed to soothe the spirits of our traumatized population quite as effectively as good old-fashioned comfort food. Many chefs talk about the pure pleasure they experience when they catch the look of delight and contentment on the faces of their customers as they taste the dishes that have been prepared for them. There's a real pride and joy around great cooking. It is a wonderful way to share, and it is a wonderful outlet for creativity. When Escoffier, the fabled father of modern cooking, set out to create a gala dessert in honor of the great Australian opera singer, Dame Nellie Melba, he gave the world Peach Melba. Not only did Dame Nellie add another jewel to her crown by being the beneficiary of such a yummy testimonial, but Escoffier added another jewel to his crown and further assured his place in history by coming up with a classic. Perhaps you'll be next. Strawberries Streisand anyone?

But as you all know by now, it takes more to succeed in the culinary world than just a love and a flair for cooking. First, you have to develop a completely comfortable foundation in the basics. For some, this means going to an accredited culinary school and working under the guidance of instructors. But even if you go this route, the real education begins when you're on your feet, in the kitchen, working on the job. And the education never ends. Whether you've gotten your start in a school, in some kind of apprenticeship program, or on the job, it is up to you to continue your training on a lifelong basis. There is so much to know and stay on top of: new trends in food, including cuisines from other cultures and vegetarian and vegan options; current nutritional information that may impact on your menu choices; the ever-increasing range and availability of organic foods; environmental issues that arise around food service, such as recycling; and, of course, all of the changes in the regulations and standards regarding food safety and handling. Keep in mind that when you prepare food for a person, you are literally taking that person's life into your hands. People die from eating the wrong foods. There is no margin of error when dealing with food handling and safety.

To succeed in this field, you will want to keep a careful eye on trends in the industry and the job opportunities that open up. If you're not happy working as a corporate chef with standard recipes, for instance, then perhaps you'll want to look into becoming a research chef or an independent chef. Maybe you'll hit upon some new food trend—whatever tomorrow's equivalents are of empanadas or scones—and want to head out to some part of the world where you've always wanted to live to open up a specialty food shop. Who knows what will work? Recently, in Brooklyn, an entrepreneurial chef opened a shop that offered nothing but a wide selection of rice puddings. His customers were lined up, convinced that they had died and gone to heaven.

The route to success in the culinary field also requires you to develop your interpersonal skills. You will have to learn how to project professionalism, which means looking the part as well as playing the part. You need to learn how to get along with others who work on your team and how to have a good relationship with the most important people in your life: your customers. That means that you will have to learn how to say no when the time comes, how to handle your emotions in a high-stress field, including how to deal with conflict and manage your anger, and much, much more.

Let us not forget either how very physical the work is in this field. No matter which position you find yourself in, as a culinary professional you are a far cry from the kind of worker who sits at a desk all day (which, of course, comes with its own set of physical problems). In the kitchen, you will be lifting heavy pots, you will be on your feet for long hours, and you may be working in very warm conditions. All of this underscores the need to learn how to best take care of yourself. And taking care of yourself also means avoiding that other occupational hazard: eating too much on the job!

The purpose of this book is to bring together tips, hints, and advice from colleagues who know what it's like to work in this field, who have had their disasters and triumphs, and who want to make your life easier. This is not the book to use to find out how to make *quenelles de brochet* or a lemon soufflé. Hopefully you will have mastered these skills in the time you've already put into your training, and there are many books that can provide you with such knowledge. This book will offer some handy information on the food front—the foolproof way to prepare a hard-boiled egg, for instance—but our focus is really on the holistic experience of being a culinary professional.

When we say "holistic," we are referring to the idea of "wholeness." Wholeness is at the heart of the term *holistic*, which means "to emphasize the organic or functional relation between the parts and the whole of something." Wholeness is, in our way of thinking, closely connected to the concept of "wellness." Wellness acknowledges the connection between mind and body and is a state in which our physical, mental, and emotional conditions are in harmony and function-ing at a high level. In adopting a holistic approach to life, we take into account the mind, the body, and the spirit, and we examine how they interact and impact on each other. To neglect one will, over time, negative-ly affect the other. We suspect that you, as a culinary professional, are familiar with the phrase "you are what you eat." In fact, this old chestnut perfectly expresses the sort of holistic orientation that we're talking about. We will be looking at "the whole you," because the wholeness of you is what is at stake, and your wellness will determine how far you can go in this field and in your life.

Another significant portion of this book will examine systems. Success in the culinary field has a lot to do with setting up systems, and your fellow professionals are brimming over with ideas that they are ready to share. Some chapters are devoted to the distinct worlds of the caterer, the pastry chefs and bakers, and those professionals who work in special situations, such as dining clubs, spas, corporate dining rooms, supermarkets, test kitchens, and so forth. No matter which culinary professional you are, however, you will be faced, on and off throughout your career, with the issues of job hunting, résumé building, networking, salary negotiation, retirement planning, and what in other fields would be called the "nuts-and-bolts" (but we'll call it the "meat-and-potatoes") of the industry. Our book concludes with chapters devoted to these issues, again filled with useful tips from those who have been there and done that.

Let's start out, however, by hearing about how people feel about their overall experiences working in the culinary field.

A Smorgasbord of Opinions

The many chefs, cooks, caterers, and kitchen personnel with whom we spoke had all kinds of fascinating things to say. We've pulled out some comments that are sweet and some that are savory.

✐ Sometimes when I get home at night and my back is killing me and I've had some dope in a plaid jacket pouring ketchup all over my gorgeous goat cheese-and-sage frittata or complaining that the tuna is "raw," I'll ask myself, "Why did you do this? Why did you go into this business when you could have become a science teacher like your brother did and had security and the summers off and people treating you with respect?" And then I remember why. I think back to sitting in my grandmother's kitchen, sipping her white Tuscan bean soup, and feeling like there was nothing more important in the world than to eat something that good. I still use my grandmother's recipe, and when I see the faces of my diners, who seem just as happy sipping it as I ever was, there's a real magic to it. A real magic that makes everything else seem insignificant . . . even jerks in plaid jackets.

✐ The thing that I love most about being in this field is that I'm never bored. Never! I wish I was bored sometimes—it might be relaxing. No, I'm only kidding. But there's a real excitement built into cooking, because cooking is really about performing, isn't it? It's full of unknowns. Just like an actor can't know what will happen when he goes onstage—will he trip over a cable? forget his lines?—so a cook doesn't know if the soufflé just won't rise for some weird reason. It keeps you on your toes!

✐ For me, the field really works, because it allows you to be creative. When I go to the market or when the vendors come around and I find the perfect chocolate peppers or incredible gooseberries or something new, like golden kiwis when they were new—then I'll know what direction I'm going in that day, and I'll just feel charged up and ready to experiment.

❧ Personally I've found myself in some very frustrating situations working in this field. I went to a top cooking school, but when I got out I found myself in a kitchen where people decorated plates with canned pineapple rings. It was a real letdown, and it's a whole long story about why I felt I had to take that job in the first place, but the point is that there's a fantasy— you're going to bring food to new heights!—and there's a reality, which may be that you're preparing food you wouldn't even want to eat. The good news is that there are more jobs around than people to fill them, so I didn't have to stay long in that one before I found something more to my liking.

❧ I don't think people, when they go into this field, understand just how much pressure there is. It's not just the pressure of getting the food onto the table, which, of course, is hard work, all the time. It's also the pressure, when you're a chef, of preparing food that *sells*. You can be a great painter, you know, and paint amazing works of art, but if nobody buys them, you'll be a starving artist. Same thing goes for being a chef. You can make fabulously inventive dishes with white truffles and skate in black butter and macadamia-crusted breasts of squab, but if nobody wants to buy them, because they're too far out or whatever, then the books won't balance at the end of the evening, and that's what the restaurant business is all about, like any other business.

❧ I went into this field because I love food, but the more I'm in it, the more I realize that it's as much about the people as the food. A restaurant is like a family—you're so intensely involved, much more than in most situations (and I've worked in the corporate world in non-food related jobs). You have to be open to people, but you also have to watch what you say, because there's a lot of stress, and the wrong words can come back to haunt you.

❧ I enjoy the challenge of staying fresh and staying ahead of the game. I feel like a sponge sometimes, taking in information and input from all kinds of sources. It's very intellectually exciting—which is not what I expected.

❧ I love the teaching aspect of being a cook. Every cook I know recognizes the need to teach younger, inexperienced cooks and pass on the tradition. To take a person who has little knowledge or skill and to turn that person into a professional is very rewarding.

❧ Cooking for me has it all. It's scientific and mathematical and creative and anthropological. When I visit a country—and I make a point of doing a lot of traveling—I feel like an explorer. I smell the cornmeal, and I set out on the track of rare tomatoes or unusual potatoes, and I taste the wine, and I always, always, always bring back new ideas.

❧ One thing about becoming a culinary professional that everyone should know is that you have a huge quality-of-life choice to make here. This business means working long hours, weekends, and holidays. You'll almost never be home for dinner with the family, and you'll likely miss all the big parties and celebrations. But to me, it's all worth it. I love my job.

❧ My greatest challenge in being a chef has been balancing my efforts between food and menu development and all the administrative work that goes with the job. I think most chefs begin their careers focused on the food and only the food. Then they begin to grow, most of the time out of necessity. The trick is to try to find the balance. Don't ever let your food suffer because you're buried in paperwork.

❧ I kind of stumbled into the field. I'm a comic book artist, and like most comic book artists in the world, there's no way on earth that I could support myself on that alone. So I had a friend who was a *sous chef* in this new restaurant near me, and he got me a job as the *garde-manger.* I prepare the cold dishes, the salads, and stuff. I really took to it, because it has a definite artistic agenda to it. Vegetables are beautiful in and of themselves, and when you're arranging them on a plate—the cherry tomatoes and the carrots and the *frisée*—well, it's just a beautiful thing. Plus I've really enjoyed the camaraderie of the kitchen. The chef is this amazing woman from Poland—everything she touches comes out to die for—and when all of these talented people are working together, with this great energy and intensity, it's like a symphony orchestra or something.

✺ Why do I love this field? Because there's really no ceiling. You're doing something that is absolutely central to people's lives—*turning out food for them to eat and enjoy*—and the better you are at it, the more successful you can become. Simple as that. I mean, just look at people like [chef] Wolfgang Puck or Emeril. You can parlay your talent into an empire. I don't know if I'm good enough or I'll ever be lucky enough to do something like that, but I do know that I have a strong entrepreneurial streak, and being in a field where you can dream big dreams is very important to me.

The Career "Menu"

Before we go any farther, we really ought to identify our audience to make sure that if you're reading this, you've found yourself with the right book. We are addressing the full range of culinary professionals—chefs, cooks, kitchen staff, and caterers. Let's have a look at what those different jobs involve.

The Kitchen Brigade

Escoffier, mentioned earlier, instituted a whole new system of operations for large hotels and restaurants, what he called "the Kitchen Brigade." In this system, everybody had a distinct task, which meant that no one duplicated anyone else's work. This system provided efficiency, safety, and an *esprit de corps*. Chances are, you are not working in as grand a kitchen as those that Escoffier ruled over. Most establishments today are far more modest in scope, and the lack of skilled workers in all of these distinct areas, along with technological advances that call for a certain consolidation, has modified the brigade system substantially. It is important, however, to understand the hierarchy that Escoffier formulated, because that will give you a good overview of just about every task that might be faced in the universe we call the "kitchen."

The members of the kitchen brigade, as designated by Escoffier, are as follows:

∾ **Chef.** The chef—which, if you didn't know, is French for "chief"—is the team leader. The chef is responsible for ordering the food items, supervising all aspects of food preparation, and developing the menu.

∾ **Sous Chef.** More French—an important language in the food world, non?—"sous" is the word for "under." The *sous chef* is the chef's second-in-command. He or she does what the chef cannot attend to, will often deal with scheduling issues in the kitchen, and will help the station chefs, also known as line cooks, or *chefs de partie*, with some of their tasks.

∾ **Station Chefs.** These are the individuals known as "the cooks." The largest kitchens will have any and all of the following station chefs:

- *Saucier.* In charge of sautéed items and sauces. The saucier is the "artist" of the kitchen.
- *Poissonier.* The fish station.
- *Rotisseur.* This station is in charge of all roasting.

- *Grillardin.* The grill station is responsible for everything grilled.
- *Friturier.* The fry station is responsible for all things fried. This position may be combined with the roast station.
- *Entremetier.* The vegetable station is responsible for soups, vegetables, starches, pastas, hot appetizers, and sometimes egg dishes.
- *Tournant.* Also known as the roundsman or swing cook. He or she will go where needed.
- *Garde-manger.* The pantry chef, responsible for cold food preparation, including salads, pâtés, and cold appetizers.
- *Boucher.* The butcher is responsible for butchering meats, poultry, and sometimes fish.
- *Pâtissier.* The pastry chef handles anything baked as well as other desserts. In the most elaborate kitchens, the pâtissier will have his or her own kitchen area and will be assisted by a **confisieur** (for candies and petit fours), a **boulanger** (breads and other non-sweet baked items), a **glacier** (maker of frozen and cold desserts) and a **decorateur** (in charge of preparing showstopping cakes and other such items).
- In any of these stations, an apprentice cook, known as a **commis,** also can be found.

This, then, is the kitchen brigade. A similar dining brigade deals with the front of the room. As we've said, it is unlikely that you will find yourself in a kitchen today that boasts a *glacier* or a *decorateur.*

Beyond the kitchen brigade, the other culinary professionals to whom we are speaking in this book include caterers and proprietors of food shops, such as "carryout" food services where customers can order a lunch or dinner to take home with them. It is important to note too that there are many other new and exciting avenues for culinary professionals to explore, as the food world becomes an increasingly important dimension of the world at large. We will not be addressing these opportunities in any detail in this book, but today's culinary professional might decide to become a *food writer*, working as a cookbook author, a restaurant critic, or a journalist; a *food stylist*, involved in the photography of food for magazines, books, film, and television; a *consultant and design specialist*, working with restaurant owners to help develop settings, ambiance, menus, and efficiency; a *salesperson* for a food manufacturer, meeting with chefs to demonstrate the best use of new products; a *teacher* in a culinary school; or a chef in one of the many research and development kitchens maintained by food manufacturers, magazines, or wherever else recipes need to be tested.

Regardless of which avenue you choose in the culinary world, there are certain universal concerns that you will encounter. As we mentioned earlier, some of these include stress and burnout, conflict with fellow workers, issues of organization and efficiency, and the need to maintain optimal health and energy. The nitty-gritty advice that fills this book—how to measure flour, how to clean a burnt skillet, how to revive wilted greens—must be put into the context of far more sweeping principles by which to start living your life and developing your career. We have devised these principles during the course of writing books for professionals in any number of vocational fields. The Seven Guiding Principles that you are about to learn are designed to help you determine what you value most in your life and how you can make room for these things.

The Seven Guiding Principles

Once you've read through the **Seven Guiding Principles,** you will want to try to keep them firmly in your mind. Depending on your personal style and habits, that might mean posting them on the wall next to where you work, keeping them in your wallet to pull out at quiet moments, writing them on an index card and sticking them in your back pocket, or putting them on a tape that you can listen to when you're in the car. Maybe you'll want to turn them into a rhyme or a song that you can chant at quiet times, or, ritually, once a day, in the morning or before you go to sleep at night. Your goal will be to develop a healthy, "holistic" perspective that will sustain you over the long run of your arduous career. Your aim is to enjoy life, have fun, and be able to remember, at the end of the day, what it is you love about your work and why you chose to go into the field in the first place.

Principle #1: Become an Active Listener

The art of listening may not be quite as important to a culinary professional as it is to an airline pilot, let's say (when an air traffic controller tells the pilot to come in the left, the pilot had better hear it!), but it's still *very* important. You are, after all, a member of a team; as such, you are turning out a product *for* someone—namely, the customer. Listening is key to your work and is, in fact, one of the most important elements in the human experience overall. The more—and better—we listen, the more we can all get out of life. In this book, you will find concrete tips on specific listening techniques, but as one of the Seven Guiding Principles, we begin with the importance of taking time out in a busy day to listen to others to really hear what they have to say. Meeting the demands of a kitchen operating at full tilt is extremely consuming and can become so overwhelming that we may even look for relief by drowning out our environment and the voices of those around us. Ironically, this drowning-out process can actually intensify the stress. You stand a far better chance of relieving your stress by keeping open the lines of communication and enjoying the possible contact and camaraderie in your relationship with your colleagues and customers. Keep in mind, however, that by communication, we mean the act of engaging with others in *real* dialogue. Real dialogue means saying what you have to say and actively listening to what others have to say to you.

Principle #2: Think Outside of the Box

If you've chosen to work with food, we probably don't have to persuade you very hard to think outside of the box. You're bound to be a creative person, always contemplating new ways to prepare salmon, showcase strawberries, liven up lettuces, and what have you. In fact, some of your concepts may be a little *too* outside of the box. Why did you ever think that vanilla and lobster would pair well? Anise and oxtail? And then there was the infamous cumin ice cream. On the other hand, you may be a creative person who feels stifled by the establishment in which you're working. Welsh rabbit? Macaroni and cheese? Turkey with bread dressing and Harvard beets? Have you died and gone to that great Horn & Hardart in the sky? However you may be feeling about your current place of employment, you will need to find ways to keep your precious creativity alive and distinctly outside of "the box." Maybe that will mean getting together, on the side, once a month with friends and just going wild in the kitchen. Perhaps you'll want to make a trip to some other part of the country or hemisphere, slip down some back alley, and knock on somebody's door to taste a spoonful of whatever that person is having for dinner. It's up to you, but the point is to pull yourself up out of your rut or bring yourself down to earth—whatever is called for. Keep in mind too that continuing education is a reliable prescription for living by our second guiding principle. As long as you're learning, you stand a very good chance of thinking outside of that box, so never stop learning.

Principle #3: Take Time to Figure Out What You Find Most Satisfying

Chances are, if you've gone into the food world, it's because you love food. Maybe it was grandma's Tuscan bean soup that turned you on, like the person we quoted earlier, or maybe you had a mother or father or a grandmother or an aunt or uncle who made world-beater cheesecake or apple pie or loin of pork stuffed with apples or chicken with molé sauce. The best part of being in the world of food *is* the food—no argument there. But that doesn't mean that if you started as a *garde-manger*, you can't end up as a sushi chef, if that's your dream. It's up to you to discover what really races your motor.

Mihaly Cziksentmihalyi, Ph.D., professor of psychology at the Drucker School of Management at Clermont Graduate University, performed a groundbreaking study with adolescents. His findings are relevant to each and every one of us. The adolescents were outfitted with beepers that went off eight times a day over the course of one week each year. Every time the beepers signaled, the adolescents would report to Dr. Cziksentmihalyi what they were doing and how they were feeling about it. Among other things, Dr. Cziksentmihalyi discovered that when his subjects were involved in activities they enjoyed, they were able to develop a sense of what he called "flow," that great feeling of energy that makes people want to continue doing what they're doing and return to it whenever possible.

In chapter 2 we offer a tool and a technique by which you can begin to figure out which activities give you the greatest sense of flow. You'll learn how to assess the way you spend your time, and you will be better equipped to gauge how you feel about what you're doing. We'll be going through your day with you in detail—before, after, and during work—and we'll show you how to make a meaningful analysis regarding where you feel the most satisfied and where you feel the least fulfilled. This kind of honest assessment represents a critical step before you move on to Principle #4.

Principle #4: Create Time for the Things You Care About

As a culinary professional, you doubtlessly have a first-hand acquaintance with what it's like to be time poor. You have a very long and tiring day; there is never much time, or even *any* time, left over for other things. But the fact is, human beings must allow time to be "recharged" if they are going to function to capacity in this world. That may necessitate shifting things around, and even though such a prospect may feel impossible to you right now, the truth is, it *can* be done. Too many of us carry around a "can't do" attitude when it comes to changing our patterns. The good news is that most of us "can do" this kind of alteration.

Suppose, for instance, that you come to an awareness that you need 30 minutes of yoga a day, no matter what else happens. Thirty minutes a day, you say? Are you mad? Where are you going to find 30 minutes a day? But hold on a moment—this is your right as a human being. Neither you nor anyone else should be allowed to take this right away. But how are you going to make that happen? That's where the alteration comes in. Perhaps you'll need to do your yoga first thing in the morning. If you live with someone, and your partner has some flexibility, then maybe you'll be able to trade jobs and chores. Maybe your partner can walk the dog, feed the baby, water the plants, or whatever while you do what you need to do for yourself. Then you can make up for it on the other end of the day. Alternatively, you might find a solution in setting your alarm a half hour earlier every day and making yourself get out of bed and onto the yoga mat.

With regard to work, you may discover that there are some tasks that you could perform outside of your usual work environment. Paperwork, for instance— could you possibly do some of it at home where you're more relaxed? Or maybe you could get into work earlier to get your paperwork out of the way so you won't have to think about it for the rest of the day. Each person's preference will be different, and none is more "right" than the other. The key is to begin thinking about how you can best meet your own needs, because when your own needs are met, you stand a better chance of meeting the needs of others.

Principle #5: Learn to Enjoy What's in Front of You

Have you ever heard of the Buddhist practice known as "mindfulness"? It is central to the religion and functions as a way to teach concentration. Those who practice mindfulness learn how to focus on what is beautiful in the here and now. Mindfulness advocates living in the moment, and learning to live in the moment is a huge help when it comes to clearing away the clutter that surrounds us all.

Ask yourself how often you think about something other than what you're doing. As a culinary professional, you probably have an innate step up on mindfulness, even if you have no idea what that is, because chances are you really love your work. Because cooking is such a sensual experience, you've probably spent much of your life "in the moment," savoring the smells and tastes of all of the wonderful things to eat. But as time goes on and stress and fatigue build up, is your attitude changing? When you wash the sand from a leek or fry sage leaves in a fruity olive oil, are you right there, in the moment, experiencing the stimuli that are acting upon your senses? Or is your mind wandering off, worrying about money or thinking about the sharp words you exchanged with your wife, husband, daughter, son, mother, or father? As you simmer your Navarin of Lamb, are you also simmering over some careless remark that a coworker made about you? Do you reach a rolling boil when someone takes your favorite wooden spoon by mistake?

No matter how much you love your work or enjoy your life, it is hard to resist the humdrum routines that we are all subject to or the trivial disappointments and frustrations that we encounter every day. The practice of mindfulness is a wonderful way to get ourselves "back into shape." When you're paring an apple, focus on the fruit, which is so beautiful that great artists throughout the centuries have tried to capture its form on canvas. Savor the aroma of a seasoned Parmesan cheese. Feel the voluptuous texture of dough in your hands. And, away from your work, continue, as best you can, this practice of mindfulness. When you're driving home, don't stress yourself by thinking about your child's school conference, your boss's moodiness, or your tax bill. Think instead about how beautiful the sky looks, the light playing on the trees, and the Mozart concerto on the radio. Be in the moment, for when you are, there are endless gifts to be uncovered.

Principle #6: Learn to Be Flexible

You don't need us to tell you that there is no such thing as a day that goes exactly according to plan. Cooking is more of an art than a science, and as any artist knows, there are many noble—and some ignoble—failures to be faced. Sauces won't come together for mysterious reasons, cakes may not rise, and egg whites can prove suddenly stubborn about being beaten. Your response in the face of these failures may be to pull out your hair and gnash your teeth, but hopefully you will choose to respond in a more healthful way. If you choose the former as your habitual path, you run the risk of forming ulcers, developing high blood pressure or colitis, or just being generally unhappy. If you take the latter path, your options are far more varied.

Try the following exercise: Think of yourself as a machine that gets things done. As a cook, you place great faith in certain machines and have a great love for those who make your life easier. You wouldn't abuse your machines, would you? No—you would treat them well. You would clean them, replace any broken parts, and keep them well oiled. Well, if you think of yourself as the ultimate machine—and in a way you are—then you can think of flexibility as the lubricant that preserves your working parts. Flexibility is the very best weapon against stress, and it will soften the sharp edges that can often factor into your interactions with others. If you sometimes feel like a rubber band ready to snap or a frayed old piece of elastic that can no longer keep up your pajamas, remember that flexibility is the thing that keeps the rubber band supple and the elastic firm and effective. Like mindfulness, flexibility is a power of the mind that you can develop and strengthen the more you practice it.

Principle #7: Prioritize

Once you understand exactly what it is you *have* to do and exactly what it is you *love* to do, you are then ready to start prioritizing so you can get rid of all of the unnecessary tasks that sap your energy and that you have come to loathe and dread. You may be quite surprised by how much choice you actually have in terms of deciding where to devote your efforts. Remember to keep track of what you actually do with your time. Ask yourself the following:

❧ "What do I need to do to take care of myself that absolutely no one else can do for me?" For example: "Do I need to soak in a hot bath at the end of a long day?" "Do I need to go out with friends in the field to cement productive networking relationships?" Or, "Do I need to take my mother out for dinner because she's lonely and I haven't seen her for a while?" These are the kinds of issues you'll have to assess through this line of questioning.

❧ "Which of my responsibilities can be put off for the moment so I can deal with them later, with no harm done?" Checking supplies might be something you could put off for a day or two, for instance. Delaying such a task might be just the thing to keep you from feeling utterly overwhelmed on an already overwhelming day.

❧ "What am I doing that someone else could be doing for me?" Look around you. Is there someone else—a young or an inexperienced person, for instance, in need of some in-the-trenches experience—who you could be utilizing to do some of your tasks, thus lightening up your load? Delegation could prove a key factor in your chances for success.

So there you have it—the Seven Guiding Principles. Think about them, look them over carefully, and return to them as needed, but don't expect to embody them and live by them overnight. It doesn't happen that way. Some people may take months or even years to internalize the lessons of these principles. Even then, most have to be vigilant about not letting old and counterproductive habits creep back into control. As time goes on, the more you practice living by these principles, the more they will become second nature. And the more that happens, the more you will be able to appreciate and enjoy a quality of life that you may not have been able to attain otherwise.

Chapter Reference

Cziksentmihalyi, M. (1991). *The psychology of optimal experience.* New York: HarperCollins.

Perfect Hard-Boiled Eggs

How can anything so basic be so elusive? When they're done perfectly, hard-boiled eggs are delicious, easy to peel, and glossy white. When they're done imperfectly, they peel poorly and leave an unattractive, pocked appearance, and overcooking can result in an unappetizing grayish-green cast. Some tips follow for getting the results you want:

- Place the eggs in a single layer in a heavy saucepan. Cover them with an inch or more of cold water.
- Use salted water. That way, should the eggs crack, the white that escapes will coagulate more rapidly, sealing the hole.

- Once the water reaches a boil, turn off the heat and cover the saucepan. Leave it alone for 10 minutes, then uncover it and run cold water over the eggs for a minute or two.
- If you want your yolks very firm, leave the eggs to cool in the water for up to a week.
- To peel the eggs, gently tap each one against a hard surface, rotating each to make a crackled pattern. Begin the peeling at the broad end, where you'll find an air pocket.
- For optimal flavor, use the peeled eggs within an hour or two.

An interesting note about eggs: they are porous, and as such they will absorb flavors, thus they can take on undesirable odors, but, thinking more positively, they can be flavored with various spices and other ingredients. For instance, if you put eggs into a bowl with a truffle, let them stand in a cool place for a few days, and then hard-boil them, you will have truffle-scented eggs. If you're a curry lover, try mixing two teaspoons of a good curry powder into a pan of cold water, and proceed with the aforementioned method.

Chapter 2

Following the Recipe

s a culinary professional, you know that one of your least favorite times is when you are following a recipe—particularly a rather elaborate one—and you suddenly lose track. Did you add the butter? How many eggs have you added to the batter? Was it three, as called for? Two? One? Suddenly, you feel quite lost. The room spins. You sit down. You try hard to concentrate, but the answers just aren't coming. Failure looms.

Most cooks have developed systems to prevent such small catastrophes. Some, for instance, always keep egg cartons around so that when they are working with dishes that call for a large amount of eggs, they can put the cracked shells into the cartons, which serve as "counters." The point, however, is that we all jump the track at some point or another. It's only human. The trouble is, being human can be painful at times.

Generally, we all try our best to just get through the day. Few of us desire to be or can afford to be divas. Most of us are simply hardworking people, out to do our jobs. When people say to us, "How are you doing?," we answer, "Fine." We may not feel "fine," but nobody wants to hear otherwise, and we don't want to go into it anyway. But in that tired exchange, something very real and valuable can get lost. The details of our day become blurred. We run the risk of becoming just as disinterested in or inattentive to what is going on in our lives as the people who keep asking us that same hollow question. Our honesty, perspective, and empathy dwindle, and we become mechanical, just going through the paces.

One of the most important messages that we hope to convey in this book is that every day of your life *is* special and deserves to be carefully and fully considered. The best way to begin this consideration of how you spend your days is to keep a record of the way you use your time. Most of us spend at least 16 out of every 24 hours a day awake and, to some degree or another, active. For many of us, those 16 hours stretch out to 17, 18, or 19 hours. In that time, much of what we do makes us feel good—or at least that's the hope. We are kept busy with activities that engage us intellectually, emotionally, physically, or spiritually. We may even be lucky enough to feel energized and happy as a result of the work we do. When that happens, we are imbued with the sense of "flow" that we talked about in the previous chapter. Unfortunately, however, many of us are involved in those waking hours in things that give us no flow whatsoever. We spend too much time performing tedious tasks that rob us of a sense of meaning or purpose.

In many cases, people do not have much choice about what they do. Dishwashers generally are not washing dishes because it gives them a sense of flow to do so. This is what they are stuck with, and they may stay stuck all of their lives. Some of us feel mired at times in the day-to-day business of taking care of life's minutiae: paying bills, doing the laundry, going grocery shopping, commuting, and chauffeuring the children around. When these tasks feel relentless, we can become dispirited. Hopefully, we can all step back a few paces and convince ourselves that we have more control over our lives than we give ourselves credit for. The trick is to begin to think about what it is we really do with our time and how we feel about what we're doing. Once we start to keep track of our activities and reflect on them, we can begin to make the necessary changes in our schedules.

The main point of this book—the very reason for its existence—is to help you focus on your life so you can simplify what you're doing and make it more satisfy-ing. To that end, it's vitally important that you look at how you spend your time, not only at work but also before and after you get to work. You'll see just how much of a direct link there is between the emotional spheres of your life.

While writing this book, we spoke with a caterer, Alicia, whose story stayed in our minds. Alicia started her own business and had made a real reputation for herself in the cultural world of Houston. She was much in demand for museum and gallery openings, recitals, opening-night parties, and such. Alicia was a kind of "superwoman." She established her catering business right after she married her college sweetheart, and when we met up with her, her daughter, Cameron, had just had her first birthday . . . with one of the most beautiful birthday cakes you've ever seen, courtesy of her mother, of course. Alicia was so on top of everything and so involved in being perfect in so many different arenas that she reached a point where she was absolutely exhausted. On Monday, her day off, she often opted to sit in front of the TV, watching old movies on one of the cable stations and eating bowls of raisin bran all day long instead of a proper meal. "It was so ironic," she recalls. "I was serving people these gorgeous meals—fresh game and the most sparkling seafood you've ever seen and sinfully rich fallen chocolate cake—but when I got home, I'd eat cereal! I was so tired and felt stretched so thin that I couldn't even try to do more than that."

Alicia's sister, Suzanne, worried that Alicia's fatigue was getting out of hand. "She was always the lively one," Suzanne recalls. "Always ready to have some fun. When I saw her this way, so washed out and listless, I knew something was wrong." Suzanne felt that Alicia might simply have overdosed on too much work and too much fabulous food. "I had gotten really into swimming," Suzanne recalls. "I went to the Y four days a week and would swim laps. One Monday, I convinced Alicia to come with me, and guess what? She got hooked on it immediately. I guess it's like a genetic thing. Maybe our great-grandmother was a mermaid."

Swimming proved a revelation for Alicia, for whom the idea of doing anything on a Monday other than vegging out was unimaginable. "I just loved it," Alicia said. "For one thing, I was using parts of my body that I never got to use before, and the parts of my body that I use way too much were getting all that hydrotherapy. Plus, I was alone in the water, and at work I'm never alone. At home I'm never alone. The pool is the only place in the world where I can be alone, where I know I'm not going to be interrupted, and where I can do some thinking. Or, better yet, no thinking at all. Just concentrate on my stroke—back and forth, back and forth."

Alicia came to realize that when you spend your days catering to the needs of other people—literally putting food into their mouths—you often run out of juice, so to speak, when it comes to taking care of your own needs. No matter how intense your job may be—and few people work in fields as intense as the restaurant business—you still need to make time for your spouse or partner, your children, your extended family, your friends, to some extent your community, and last, but hardly least, yourself. You need to set aside time to grow your garden, paint your watercolors, groom your dog, swim your laps, or do whatever it is that races your motor and/or calms your spirit.

You are a multifaceted person—don't forget that. And don't let your work turn you into a one-dimensional person.

Now all of the aforementioned should not be interpreted as a stern warning against vegging out in front of the TV when you need to. Hey, there comes a time when nothing beats a pint of coffee ice cream, a recliner, and an old Bette Davis movie. There is a time and a place for everything, and our purpose in this book is not to pass judgment or establish rules. If it's veg-out time for you and *All About Eve* is on, then just fasten your seatbelt and go for a nice long ride, if that's what you need. But if watching television, sleeping a lot, or eating too much is leaving you feeling even more tired and drained, if you're starting to sense that these passive activities are sapping your energy, then that means that it's probably time for you to experiment with another kind of activity so you can find the release you're really looking for.

 *Keeping Track*

In order to develop an awareness of how you spend your day—and how you *feel* about how you spend your day—we are going to suggest an assignment. The pages that follow in this chapter can serve as a kind of workbook. The headings include:

- **Start/Stop/Total**
- **Activity**
- **Feelings**

- **Efficiency**
- **What's My Role?**

End-of-Day Analysis

Copy the above headings into a notebook that is small enough for you to carry comfortably throughout the day. A small, spiral-bound pad that can be tucked into your coat or jacket pocket for easy access would be perfect. Your goal is to create a journal or log that reflects exactly what you do with your time during any given day. This exercise works particularly well if you keep at it for an entire week, or even beyond. Doing so enables you to keep track of your weekends, which for most culinary professionals are particularly intense, and to determine whether, in fact, you even have a "weekend." If not, then as you keep your journal, you'll have to determine whether there *is* a time during the week when you are free. If you can't locate such a time, what does that mean for you as a person, and what can you do about it?

Now we recognize that it may prove difficult for you to find the few moments necessary during your intensely busy day to log your activities. When you're in the middle of carving a roast or piping meringue onto a Baked Alaska, it may not feel like the right time to whip out your little notebook to start recording. Certainly the point of this exercise is to make your life easier, not more difficult, so just do what you can. Whenever you come up for air, jot down your notes. If you can, try to glance at your watch so you can make a mental note of the time you begin and end an activity. The actual jotting-down part can always come later.

So then, without further ado, we now explain how to go about doing what we're asking you to do.

Start/Stop/Total

Okay now—are you ready to take a good look at your day? Are you prepared to feel proud of how quickly you managed to deal with that salesperson who came by today, trying to sell you the world's best ready-made stock? Are you ready to feel not so proud of those hours you didn't get to spend with your child, spouse, or partner—that so-called "quality time" that never happened?

Again, a reminder: In order for you to take stock of your day, you're going to have to be conscious of the clock, from the moment your alarm goes off in the morning until you close your eyes at night. Think about the many distinct activities that make up your day: getting dressed; taking care of your houseplants and your canary; catching up on your correspondence; reviewing the day's menus and making alterations and adjustments based on last-minute discoveries and dis-appointments from the vendors; actual food prepara-tion; long-term planning; advertising and promotion, if you get involved with that; networking . . . the list goes on. Each time you begin a new activity, jot down the "start" time. Do the same when you finish that activity—note the "stop" time—before you move on to your next one. Don't forget to factor in downtime like "deep breathing," or whatever. As for the "total time spent," you can worry about that later. You don't need to burden yourself with adding, subtracting, and justifying yourself in the middle of your crazy day. This exercise is just a matter of putting down straight numbers—10 minutes to walk the dog; 25 minutes to get to work; 4 minutes to prepare the persillade; 6 minutes for the pico de gallo—and you can easily tally it at the end of the day.

Some of your colleagues who have gone through this part of the regimen have said the following:

✧ This **Start/Stop/Total** exercise is a real eye-opener. It makes you look at your whole day and see what you've managed to get done and what you haven't done. I wound up feeling like even though I think I'm time-poor, I've actually got more time available to me than I thought I did.

✧ If you really follow the assignment and do what you're supposed to do, you'll soon discover your patterns, and then you can decide whether you want to keep them or not. For instance, after four or five days, I realized that I was talking to my boyfriend for over an hour every day. He's a computer geek and works at home and can multitask like you wouldn't believe, so, for him, talking on the phone is no biggie. But, for me, it's time away from the time I have when I'm not working . . . and, being a pastry chef for a big hotel, there isn't much time when I'm not working. I'm not worried about our relationship—I think we're really solid and don't need to talk to each other so much on the phone—so that's a place where I think I can cut back. Like, we can talk on the phone maybe 10 minutes twice a day and I think that would work fine.

ᕧ Doing this exercise showed me stuff that was so obvious, it's like, why didn't I see that? For example, I walk my dog 15 minutes a day, and I exercise 45 minutes a day. So I said to myself, hey, Einstein, you could exercise by walking the dog! I could save myself *hours* a week doing that, and I could put those hours to good use somewhere else.

Activity

Once you start filling in your activity chart, you'll see how many different hats you wear during any given day. You may see yourself as a parent (bought scooter for Bobby), as a child (took mom to the airport), as a friend (going-away party for Sasha), as a lover (dinner at Julio's), as an employee (reorganized spices), as a neighbor (picked up prescription for Mrs. Jackson), as a cook (made orange crème brulee), and more. Your **Activity** entries will help you focus on all of these "hats." The more specific you are in noting which category your activity falls into, the more you'll learn from the information in your log at the end of the week. If you are consulting with a customer about which flavor of icing to use for a wedding cake, then make note of it. If you are involved in a staff meeting to get to the bottom of the missing Callebaut chocolate, then make note of it also. Don't let anything slip by. It all counts.

When you're working on your log, keep in mind that this is for your eyes and your eyes only. You are the sole contributor and the only one who will be reading this. The goal is to learn about yourself, how you spend your time, and how you feel during the day. Some colleagues made the following comments:

✐ It was interesting, because I realized that I was spending more time on activities I don't particularly enjoy, like scheduling, instead of activities that I do enjoy, like cooking. It got me thinking that I'll probably have to make some changes in order to get to do more of what I like to do. It may even necessitate changing jobs—we'll see.

✐ One thing that felt good about doing this was seeing how much I manage to get done. Work, taking a workshop on new Asian cooking, helping my kid with her science project . . . I'm a great juggler!

Feelings

Soon after you've finished an activity, do your best to jot down your feelings about it. By doing so now, your feelings will be more honest, and you will be less inclined to edit them, either consciously or unconsciously. It isn't important to write down long, detailed notes at this point. A few well-chosen words will do just fine. A good way to begin is to think in terms of "feeling" words: are you happy, sad, angry, bored, or worried? Next, try thinking in terms of opposites— happy or sad; relaxed or tense; worried or optimistic; loving or angry; gentle or tough; energetic or tired; interested or bored—and judging which of the two poles you feel closer to in each instance.

Your goal in this section is to gauge how much satisfaction you're getting out of your activities. Most of us have to do things that aren't exactly rewarding, but certain aspects of these activities can still bring us satisfaction. For instance, you may have to grate lemon peel . . . but you love your new Microplane® grater that makes such short order of this work. You might have to bring soup tonight to your ailing uncle way over on the other side of town . . . but you'll be gratified by the expression on his face when he tastes it. You may have to repair the tear in your uniform . . . but you can catch up on a favorite soap opera while you do it. Keeping a record of the feelings you experience during the day will help you identify the things that give you pleasure and the things that don't, and if certain patterns emerge—anything you do to music, for instance, comes easier to you—then you'll have discovered something important about yourself.

Remember not to think too hard or long when you write down your reactions. Your gut response is probably the most reliable. Again, keep in mind that this log is for your eyes only, so don't worry about what others will think when you record your honest reactions. Here is what one of our culinary professionals had to say about this exercise:

✑ I enjoyed this part. A few summers ago, I actually took off a few weeks and had some serious R & R at a retreat. One of the things we did there was journaling, and this reminded me of that. I'm a chef in a small but very busy restaurant in San Francisco, and like chefs everywhere, I often run the risk of getting totally overwhelmed. Doing this part of the log forced me to identify the feelings I have about different aspects of my work—managing other people, for instance, as compared to creating menus—and it was interesting to see, in so many words, what I felt about those different aspects.

Efficiency

As a culinary professional, you are well aware of the need for efficiency. Every minute counts in this field, and a tool that is not sharp enough, a beater that doesn't have enough power, or a package that is a pain in the neck to open is a devilish inconvenience conspiring to make your life more difficult. One of the most important concepts that a culinary professional learns, after all, is *mise en place* (the French term meaning "to put in place," or "everything in its place"). Essentially, the concept of *mise en place*, as formulated by Escoffier, mentioned in chapter 1, suggests that a chef should have everything on hand that he or she will need to prepare and serve food in an organized and efficient fashion. So being imbued with the concept of *mise en place*, you, as a culinary professional, will have a particular sensitivity to matters of efficiency. Even so, it is important to keep in mind that efficiency is *not* the highest ideal in the world. Yes, it is important, and yes, you are taught modes of efficiency as a culinary student, but admit it—you've known great chefs who haven't been models of efficiency, isn't that so? And there also is the phenomenon of the person who is a model of efficiency in the kitchen but other areas of her or his life are a veritable pigpen. This may, in fact, be preferable to the person who takes the concept of *mise en place* beyond the kitchen and becomes such a control freak in every area of life that if his or her partner should move the remote control to the TV a quarter-inch to the right of where it's usually kept, then Monsieur or Madame *Mise en Place* totally freaks out!

Where are you on the efficiency spectrum? Are all of your wooden spoons lined up like toy soldiers, ready to do battle, while your handbag is a repository for used tissues and car wash coupons? Or are you a mad genius who throws around pots and pans in pursuit of the perfect *pots de crème*, wholly insensitive to the mess you're making for others? Now's the time to start paying attention to your habits. You may be surprised—and chastened—by the role that efficiency, or lack of it, is playing in your life.

When addressing this subject in your log, keep in mind that there may be instances where efficiency really doesn't apply. For example, if you are looking at the time of day when you take a bath, efficiency doesn't necessarily enter into that picture. It might be more "efficient" for you to take your bath in four minutes, rub-a-dub-dub. On the other hand, it might be better for you, in the bigger picture, to take a half-hour bath, just lying and soaking away the stress of the day. You be the judge. And if you determine that efficiency does not apply to a given task, then simply write N/A (not applicable) in your log. Otherwise, make an effort to rate your efficiency in any given activity on a 1 to 5 scale. This exercise was an eye-opener for some of our culinary professionals:

✐ After keeping the log, I saw how inefficient I was in some areas of my life. Like shopping for myself, for instance. I always just think about food at work, and at home I'm constantly running out of things like coffee and milk and juice. Pretty stupid, eh?

✐ I took a look at my log at the end of the week, and I went, whoa! You *are* a control freak, man. Lighten up.

What's My Role?

As we've suggested, over 24 hours, you, like most other people in the world, play a variety of roles. Not only are you a culinary professional, but maybe you're a parent, brother, sister, child, grandchild, choir member, political activist, Little League coach, or bird-watcher . . . well, you get the idea. It is useful to think about which of these roles you most enjoy and which of them suit you best. For instance, as a chef, not only do you prepare food and devise menus but chances are you enact the role of teacher as you help your fellow kitchen staff understand a dish that you've created. Think about the roles you play and then, during a given week, compile a list of these roles somewhere in the back of your notebook or pad. As you fill in your log, figure out which roles you've been playing for which activity, but don't feel that you have to record these close to the time of the activity. This category and the next—**End-of-Day Analysis**—can be filled in when you find some quiet time.

	ACTIVITY #1	ACTIVITY #2	ACTIVITY #3
Start			
Stop			
Total			
Feelings			
Efficiency			
What's My Role?			

End-of-Day Analysis

Now for the *pièce de resistance!* The very last thing you do each day, just before you turn out the lights, is analyze your log. This is your opportunity to learn something about yourself, and believe it or not, for many people the results are genuinely surprising. Follow these steps:

1. Begin by totaling the first row, **Start/Stop/ Total.** Add up the total for each activity, and note it.

2. Review what you've written in the **Activity** column, and read down the column to **What's My Role?** Think about what your role has been in each activity, and note it in the appropriate place.

3. When you've filled in the entire **What's My Role?** column, check back to the **Feelings** column and think about which roles you found most pleasurable or satisfying. Note as well those activities you found least pleasurable or satisfying. Give yourself time to think about how you might rearrange your life to maximize time spent in the pleasurable roles and minimize time spent in those roles you do not enjoy.

4. Look back at your **Start/Stop/Total** column, and match it with the **Feelings** column. How much time did you spend doing the things that offered you little satisfaction? How much time did you spend doing the things you most love to do?

5. Think about what was most surprising in your log, and make a note of it. Perhaps it was how much time you spent doing things that you genuinely do not enjoy. Or, maybe—hopefully—it was the other way around. Maybe you're surprised by how much pleasure you took in the more scientific aspects of your work—the

mathematical calculations, for instance. Maybe you were surprised by how interested you were in being interviewed by the food writer who asked you to describe the kind of cooking you do.

6. Repeat this process every day for a week, each day with a new log. At the end of the week, go over all of your notes, paying special attention to the **End-of-Day Analysis.** Give yourself ample time to think about what you are reading.

Again, the goal here is to reflect. Ultimately, you want to find enough time in your life to do more of what you love and less of what you don't. To achieve that goal, you need to keep track of the following **Seven Guiding Principles,** discussed in chapter 1.

1. Become an active listener.
2. Think outside of the box.
3. Take time to figure out what you find most satisfying.
4. Create time for the things you care about.
5. Learn to enjoy what's in front of you.
6. Learn to be flexible.
7. Prioritize.

Keeping a log and being mindful of the Seven Guiding Principles is only one step toward making the most of your life as a culinary professional. The next chapter will introduce you to the very important issue of organizing—the things around you and your life in general.

How to Cook Pasta

Overcooked pasta? What a dreadful notion. Nothing would seem simpler than cooking pasta, but in fact some restaurant kitchens don't get it right every time, which is unaccountable and inexcusable. This procedure, as is the case with those throughout the book, is geared for the small kitchen. You will have to figure out the adaptations for larger operations. The basic approach follows:

- Bring four quarts of water to a rolling boil in a six-quart or larger stockpot or Dutch oven.
- Add one and one-half teaspoons of salt and one pound of dried pasta. (Note that it is not necessary to add oil to the cooking water, as some cooks do.)
- Stir to separate the pasta.
- Cover the pot, and return to a boil. Remove the cover when the water is boiling, and stir frequently to keep the pasta separate.
- Taste for doneness three minutes prior to when the box says it is done. If the pasta is still hard, continue to taste test it every 30 seconds until it is just *al dente*.
- Remember to reserve some of the pasta cooking water if needed for your recipe, and then drain the pasta in a large colander, allowing it to sit, without shaking, for 30 seconds. Rinse the pasta only if you are planning to use it in a salad; otherwise,

the sauce will not adhere to it as well. Continue with your recipe.

Fresh pasta is treated just as dried pasta is, but it will take considerably less time to cook—just minutes, in most cases, so don't wander away from the stove. There are different schools of thought about which pasta is superior—dried or fresh. Many chefs like to use dried pasta for meaty sauces, as it is firmer and denser and holds up better to such a treatment. They reserve fresh pasta for delicate sauces, such as those using cream bases and fresh tomatoes.

Chapter 3

Everything In Its Place

In the previous chapter, we referred to the concept of *mise en place*—everything in its place—and in this chapter we will be offering some advice about how to achieve *mise en place* in the kitchen. However, we also would like to apply the concept to other areas of your life, outside of the kitchen. So in the context of this chapter, "everything in its place" will be synonymous with "everything organized." We will be asking you to assess the kind of personality you have and what organization means to you. How far will you go to attain organization? Will you stop at nothing to have your socks neatly laid out in your drawers? Or are you a happy-go-lucky sort, the kind who depends on a string wrapped around your finger to remind you of important events?

Whatever your orientation is toward organization, by the end of this chapter, you will hopefully make the connection between organization and time management. The more organized you are, the more time you will have to relax, to explore, to improve yourself, to get closer to others, and more. It will be your choice how to use your extra time, but won't it be nice to have that option?

In the Kitchen . . .

Let's start with some "meat and potatoes"—the issue of *mise en place* in the kitchen. As we said, this concept is central to the life of a culinary professional. It means having everything at the ready when you prepare a dish. Your colleagues say the following on this topic:

✑ First things first—read the recipe! That's the most elementary advice I could give anyone, and the best. I have found that most mistakes in the kitchen are made because people don't read their recipes through before they start.

✑ Naturally, you'll want to round up all your ingredients before you get going. You want to make sure that everything is fresh and vital. Obviously, anything perishable has to be evaluated, but also herbs and spices might be past their prime.

✑ Consider everything you're about to do, and check to see what you can double up on. For instance, if several of your recipes call for chopped cilantro or grated lime zest, prepare as much as you'll need for all the dishes in one fell swoop. That's the way to save time in the kitchen.

‿ Don't waste time measuring out everything before you start. Most things, yes, but when it comes to stuff likes oils and vinegar, you can simply pour these from the bottle as you go.

‿ Like everything else in life, it's all about the effort you make. In cooking, there are legitimate shortcuts, and then there's just plain sloppiness and laziness. When you're prepping your ingredients, don't do half a job. If you're using spinach or leeks in your dish, for instance, spend the necessary time to make sure that every last grain of sand goes down the drain. If that means multiple washings, then so be it. And you can plan ahead with that kind of job. You can get your veggies done way in advance and just have them in the fridge, all ready to go.

‿ I always like to keep a large tray handy to hold all my ingredients in pinch bowls or ramekins. That way, I'm kind of mobile. I can pick up the tray and take my stuff to another station in the kitchen if I need to.

‿ Hey, I don't know what Escoffier would have to say about this, but I like to use disposable muffin tins or coffee filters for my *mise en place*. I put my ingredients in these, and when I'm finished, they go into the garbage. Nothing to clean!

‿ Clean as you go. That's the motto. *Mise en place* doesn't just mean having all your ingredients and tools in place. It also means putting your scraps where they belong.

The Right Stuff

Maybe you're lucky enough to work in a kitchen that is inventoried with all of the equipment you'll ever need. Then again, maybe you're not so lucky. In fact, maybe you're setting up your own kitchen for a carryout shop or a catering concern. In any case, a critical aspect of *mise en place* is making sure that you have the right tools for the job. A list of tools that all cooks will want to keep handy at all times follows:

- baster
- basting brush
- box grater
- garlic press
- metal fry basket
- cheesecloth
- colanders in various sizes (including at least one with a handle)
- meat tenderizer (mallet)
- metal tongs
- skimmer (for defatting soups, etc.)
- scraper (for scraping up dough)
- pinch bowls (small bowls used to hold spices, herbs, citrus zests, and so on). These can be improvised if necessary out of jars (baby food jars are good) or other small containers.
- marble mortar and pestle

- assorted wooden spoons
- metal and rubber spatulas
- mixing bowls

These are just the basics, of course. Your dream kitchen also will include things such as baking stones, a pizza pan and wheel, a pastry crimper, and much, much more, not to mention appliances such as food processors, standing mixers, and so forth.

. . . And Out of the Kitchen

We could spend all day talking about organizational tips in the kitchen, and more of these will be integrated throughout this book, but we return now to the central "organizing" idea of this book, which is that we are human beings *in a context*, and we can only benefit by viewing ourselves holistically. We're not just chefs or *sous chefs* or pastry chefs or kosher caterers or candy makers. Those are important elements of who we are, but first and foremost, we are people—people with very full lives—and so, as promised, we extend the metaphor of *mise en place* to your life in general. Do you feel as though you have "everything in place," or do you feel more like Atlas with the world resting on your shoulders, staggering under the weight of it all? As a culinary professional, not only do you have the stress of always having to "perform," but also you may have a rotating schedule, which never really allows you to fall into a comfortable sense of familiarity and ease. Most likely, you'll also be working late nights, which can be another form of stress. The solution to these on-the-job difficulties is to make yourself as organized as possible (although keeping in mind that the extent to which you are organized must also be consistent with your innate personal style).

Becoming organized and managing your time is part art, part science, and part pure determination. Even if your basic nature were not to be all that organized, most of us would agree that there is significant room for improvement. Consider the tips that follow from your colleagues in the field, and start thinking about how you can put some of their ideas into practice.

Time Management

Surely you've heard the expression "Time heals all wounds," but are you familiar with its inverse—"Time wounds all heels"? Both expressions are reflections of the ambivalent feelings that characterize most people's relationship to time. Time is a fact of life—as elemental as the weather—but our feelings about it can be extremely complicated. The issue of time and how it impacts on us has the capacity to be wounding, frustrating, and highly confusing. Those of us who tend to be chronically late try the patience of friends, family, and coworkers. On the other hand, those of us who are obsessively punctual and who fail to understand that time is not always "of the essence" run the risk of being characterized as martinets. Time also is a culturally sensitive issue. In certain cultures, scheduling is obsessive and fanatical. In other cultures, deadlines are barely adhered to. A notorious example of a clash of cultures occurred when Germany and Italy became allies during World War II. The Germans, who had scheduling down to a fine science, threw up their hands in despair over the Italians, whose Mediterranean concept of time was decidedly casual. So then, as they say, there's no time like the present to start talking about time and what it means to you.

It's About Time

Time, as we say, is both absolute and relative. Let's hear what your fellow culinary professionals have to say on the subject.

✐ I refuse to let time rule my life. Some cooks walk around with a minute timer, even when they're not cooking something. It gets pretty crazy. I don't want to live that way.

✐ I know chefs, particularly French and Italian ones, who laugh at the American obsession with time. When we ask them how long it takes to bake a certain dish, they say, "As long as it takes," and they will absolutely refuse to be tied down to actual cooking time.

☞ I give cooking demonstrations to amateurs, and the thing that so many of them are crazed about is the cooking time. I have to explain that cooking time varies, based on the oven and other factors. But it makes them feel so insecure.

☞ My father was in the military, and time was always this big deal in our family. Heaven forbid you should ever be late for something. Now, at this point in my life, as an adult, I carry a clock around inside of me, and I think that's a much better way to live. I get up the same time every day, without an alarm clock, and I don't need a timer to tell me when an egg's hard-boiled, because I have a *sense* of time. I think that's a comfortable way to live in this world—to have an inner sense of time, an inner organizer. Otherwise, you're always watching the clock.

☞ To me, the curse of modern life is that we're all so overscheduled. It's like everyone's running around with their organizers and their cell phones, and heaven forbid you might be a little late getting somewhere! It's such a one-sided way of looking at life. I try to have a sense of what I need to do generally—I need to go to the Food Show on Monday, I need to buy my mother a Mother's Day gift, I need to get to my dental cleaning—but even with these goals in mind, I still want to have some feeling of flexibility. If there's a solar eclipse, or even a rainbow, I want to be able to stop and look at it. If I'm sitting in a café with some person having an incredible, life-altering conversation, I don't want to have to jump up at 11:43 because the dog has to be walked. You know what I mean?

Getting a Handle on It

Okay—so we agree that time is a complicated issue. How do we get started on making our peace with it? Try out the following ideas from your fellow culinary professionals:

✒ As a chef-owner of a small restaurant, I am constantly teetering on the brink of being completely overwhelmed. Part of what overwhelms me is that I have so many people asking me for things. I'll have a customer who's in the advertising business, and he wants to create a TV spot for me. Well, I just can't swing that right now, but even so, there I am, still agreeing to meet him for coffee to discuss it. Why? Because I haven't learned how to say no yet. And if you think about it, the issue of time management is very much linked to the issue of assertiveness. If you can't learn to say no, then people are always going to be taking advantage of you and using up your time however they see fit.

✒ I've come to [the] realization that I just have to be direct with people, almost to the point of rudeness. When I'm catering a wedding and there's some kind of crisis starting up, like there always is, if someone calls me on my cell who can't tell me at that exact moment where I'm going to get a bunch of white violets for my celebration salad, then I'm just not going to talk to that person. I don't care if it's my mother or Laura Bush or the *New York Times*. Because if I don't say no, I know I'm just going to get myself into a whole mess of trouble.

 Some people can handle interruptions better than other people. I don't do interruptions very well. When I'm piping buttercream roses onto my cake, I don't want to hear from anyone just then. So I let people know I'm unavailable. When I'm finished, I'll entertain questions, I'll take phone calls—whatever. Just don't try to come between me and my buttercream roses.

 I "give" people time. I think of it as my little gift to them. If my mother suddenly wants to talk to me about this outfit she saw on sale at the department store, I say, "Okay, Ma, you've got five minutes." If my friend Diane calls up to ask me whether she should color her hair red, I'll say, "Okay, Di, you've got five minutes." Five minutes is as much of a gift as I want to give anyone when I've got so much pressure on me to get things done.

Making Lists

Most people find that the best way to get a handle on time is to keep a "to do" list. Okay, so maybe you don't think of yourself as a "list" sort of person. But would you go to a supermarket without a shopping list? No—you wouldn't trust your memory. The same principle applies to a to-do list, which not only reminds you of what you need to do but organizes you in the bargain. Keeping this list goes a long way toward moving your days from chaos to control. Whether you use a memo pad, a pocket calendar, an electronic organizer, a stick-it pad, or a ballpoint pen on the palm of your hand, don't leave home without it! And once you start keeping a daily to-do list, you also may find a weekly or even a monthly list beneficial. Tips from your colleagues follow:

✐ I've been keeping a to-do list for a couple of years now, and it's made a big difference in my life. I've gotten into the habit of starting my day off by reviewing my list. I'll sit down with a cup of coffee and, if my waistline can afford it, a slice of toasted farm bread with my own strawberry jam, and I'll look it over really carefully. If I can do this in a relatively peaceful, calm moment, I feel like I've got half the battle won. At least I'm starting out with some kind of battle plan for the day, and that's worth a lot.

✐ There's one rule I never break, and if you're smart, you might want to do the same: keep your to-do list to one side of one page. If you've got a to-do list that can't fit on one side of one page, that means you've got too much "to do"! Also, unless you're the kind of person who does crossword puzzles in pen, always write your to-do list in pencil, because you know it's going to change. That's the nature of a to-do list—it's a work in progress. Things get canceled and shuffled around all the time . . . particularly when you do the kind of work that we do.

✐ Everybody's got his or her own method, but my "sanity secret" is to schedule in at least one block of free time a day. No matter how packed the day is that's coming up, I'll still factor in free time. That way I've got protection in case something unexpected comes along, like car trouble or my dog running away or whatever. And something unexpected always does come up, doesn't it?

✎ Check off your to-do list as you go along. Put a big red line through each item. It feels good to check those little buggers off and to see how much you're getting done!

Prioritization

The organizational principle of *prioritization*—attacking tasks in the order of their importance—is critical when making lists. Your fellow culinary professionals say the following:

✎ A to-do list doesn't make sense unless you prioritize it. You need to put the most important thing at the top of your list. ORDER THE TURKEYS . . . if Thanksgiving is coming up. At the bottom is where you want to put the stuff that you'd like to do, but if you never get around to it, no one will notice. CLEAN GROUT AROUND THE SINK, for instance.

✎ How do you figure out priorities? Here's what I do. I look at the items on the list, and I ask myself what good or bad things will happen if I do or don't get them done. Like if I have to interview someone to fill a kitchen staff position, I know that if I don't do that and I don't fill the job, everyone else, including me, will have to work a lot harder—bad thing. On the other hand, if I find someone great to fill the job today, then I won't have to do any more interviewing for the rest of the week—good thing.

🌀 Here's a hot tip: finish one task before you go on to the next. In other words, if you've prioritized your to-do list, as you should have, you don't go on to the #4 priority until you've got #1 squared away.

Organizers

Nothing makes your life easier—and nothing makes you more reliable—than a good organizer. Of course, recommending an organizer is a little like recommending a brand of shampoo. Is your hair dry, curly, or fine? Do you spend a lot of time outdoors? Similarly, when you recommend an organizer, you have to keep the person in mind. Is she or he technologically challenged? Does he or she tend to lose things a lot? How far along the organizational path has she or he come? Is the whole idea of having "a book" foreign? Does the person have to start out small? Your fellow culinary professionals prefer the following organizers:

🌀 I laugh when I see all the equipment that the people I work with use. I am Spanish, from a little town in the mountains, and I do not feel the need to have all that equipment. For me, a pencil and pad is enough.

🌀 I need a week-at-a-glance and a month-at-a-glance. I need to see the big picture.

🌀 I got so good at keeping a daily to-do list that I figured I'd start thinking bigger, and so now I keep a weekly to-do list too. This way, I can try to organize myself for bigger chunks of time. If I have something important looming due ten days ahead, I can see it coming. Next step is the monthly list!

🍥 How can anyone *not* use an electronic organizer these days? Whether it's a Palm Pilot® or a Handspring® or any of the knockoffs, to me the difference between an electronic organizer and a regular old date book is like the difference between a computer and a typewriter. You can program in birthdays, all kinds of information about customers and vendors, and you can set alarms for yourself through the day to remind yourself to baste the turkey or turn the roast or whatever—it's incredible!

🍥 In our kitchen, we use a "communal" organizer as well as our own individual ones. We've got a big hanging board with erasable dry-ink markers, and it serves kind of like the big board in an emergency room. All the cooks, like all the doctors in the ER, know what their jobs are on any given day and where they're supposed to be.

Winning at Organization

Organization seems to breed more organization. In a sense, it's a kind of worldview. You start coming up with all kinds of ways to save time. What follows is a grab bag of good ideas from your fellow culinary professionals about where and how you can find those precious moments.

As a caterer, I find that making phone calls, even routine ones, eats up a huge amount of my time, so I try to return calls when people are inclined to be more brief. For instance, I often get calls from a florist who works with us, and she's a lovely woman, but boy is she a talker! It's almost impossible for me to get off the phone with her. So I try to call at odd hours when I figure she won't be in or she'll be on the run, like right before breakfast when I get her machine or just before lunch when she'll be heading out.

Making phone calls definitely is a drag on your time. I return all my calls in one block. I give myself an hour a day to do it—no more, hopefully less. But doing them all together makes it more of a job so you don't get carried away with any one person.

You want to know my secret to saving time? Find people to help you. Sometimes that costs money, and only you can decide if you can afford it and if it's worthwhile. Other times you have to weigh the money against the kind of money you could make if you had that time at your disposal. For instance, if you hate cleaning house and you're paying somebody $10 an hour to do it, can you make $15 an hour in that time you'd be vacuuming? If so, it's a no-brainer. And then there are opportunities that won't cost you a cent, like using a travel agent to book a trip instead of trying to do it yourself.

I think it's really important to be sensitive to your actual work environment and to see how you can save precious minutes and precious energy just by making physical changes. Are your wooden spoons in easy reach, or are you stretching for them? Dish towels? Spatulas? You want to set things up so your life is as easy as it can be.

✑ Pre-plan and attend to as many details as you can in advance. If you're doing a cooking demonstration somewhere the next day, for instance, have your wardrobe laid out, all pressed and cleaned, the night before. If you're going to be depositing a check or you're going to the theater the next day, put the check or your tickets in your wallet at night. There are always way too many things to do in any given day. If you can get a jump on things the night before, you'll see the difference.

✑ Tell yourself that every minute counts. Let's say you're going out to lunch with a food writer in five minutes. Don't look at it as if you've only got five minutes so why should you start something? You can make a phone call in five minutes and get that out of the way. You can meditate for five minutes, if you know how, and feel refreshed and ready for your interview. The real merit of being organized is that you get to take advantage of *every* minute.

The Lost and Found of Time

If, over the next few weeks, you keep close tabs on how you use your time, then our guess is that you'll be shocked by how much of it slips through your fingers.

All of us can save hours a week just by becoming aware of certain little shortcuts and "fast ones" that we can pull on old Father Time. The following tips will give you some ideas of ways to own your time again in the many areas of your life.

Travel

As a culinary professional, you may find yourself doing quite a bit of traveling. After all, a good cook is always in demand. Here are some organizing tips collected from your colleagues to make your business travel easier:

✎ Keep a master checklist of all your travel needs. You should have boxes you can check off for your alarm clock, money belt, shampoo, allergy pills, and so forth. Before you take off on a trip, check your list to make sure you have everything.

✎ When you're packing your suitcase, write down a list of everything that's going into it. That way, if your luggage is lost, you'll know what's missing.

✎ Get a good map and a road guide to where you're going *before* you get there. Maps can be difficult to obtain. You don't want to get stuck. At worst, print out directions to all of your meetings on Mapquest <http://www.mapquest.com> before you leave.

✎ One of the best things you can do for yourself when you travel is to restrict your luggage to one carry-on bag. That way, you can skip the long waits at the carousel and the running after the airlines when they lose your bags.

🌱 I like to bring my own pillow with me when I travel. At least I'll know that I can get a good night's sleep that way. I also throw a night-light into my bag. I've stayed in hotels where the rooms are pitch black at night, and I don't feel like breaking my neck (or my shins) in the dark.

🌱 Keep all of your receipts together if you're going to be putting in for reimbursement or claiming deductions for tax purposes.

🌱 Always carry an extra pair of eyeglasses with you . . . that's assuming you need eyeglasses.

Good Habits Start at Home

You can be super-organized at work, but if you don't follow through on the home front, you'll have problems aplenty. Some ideas from your fellow professionals include the following:

🌱 I systematically get rid of things once or even twice a year. Anything that's broken, anything with a leg missing, anything that I've been holding onto thinking that one day I might be able to replace a part . . . that all gets thrown away. All the clothes that I can no longer fit into or that I never should have bought in the first place . . . thrown away. You know what I'm talking about. Cleaning the debris out of your life is the quickest and straightest path to real organization.

🌱 For years I'd drive myself crazy looking for things. My wallet, my keys, my eyeglasses. Why did I put myself through such misery? Now I put everything in one place, right in my kitchen, in a cookie jar. As soon as I come home at night, there it all goes. Not looking for things has bought me so many hours to use on stuff that's a lot more pleasant.

✑ I refuse to spend precious moments of my life going through junk-mail and junk e-mails, so I do whatever I can to get myself removed from lists. You know, if they don't do what you ask, they can be severely fined, so just make a little noise and those pests will run away with their tails between their legs.

✑ My key to being organized is to have one secret place in my house—one big closet—that's a total mess. Everyone needs a pocket of mess in their lives, or otherwise they're like Martha Stewart, you know? It's where you put all the stuff you don't know what to do with but that you aren't ready to throw away.

✑ Magazines are my pet peeve. It drives me crazy to see all those magazines piling up unread. I start to feel like I have this enormous burden to take care of. But a friend of mine gave me a great idea. What she does is this: as soon as she gets a magazine, she leafs through it. If there's nothing there that jumps out at her, she throws it in the garbage. If there are one or two articles or a recipe or a book review or whatever, she'll immediately clip the thing she's interested in, stick it in an accordion folder, and toss the rest of the magazine. It's a great way to keep down the clutter.

✑ I keep a wastebasket in every room. It encourages me, in an ongoing way, to get rid of stuff and keep down the clutter. If you have to walk all the way to another room down the hall to throw something away, it's not going to happen.

✐ I do this little obsessive thing that people make fun of me for, but I think it really works. Whenever I leave one room, I look around and take something that I know belongs somewhere else. And believe me—I never fail to find something. Maybe it's a coffee cup or a spoon or a book or whatever, but the point is that I just do this in a totally ongoing way and that cuts down on my overall cleaning time.

✐ I keep cheap vacuums on every level of the house. It translates into less work for me.

. . . And Even More Ways to Save Time

Once you get into the habit of being an organized person, you'll see how many ways there are to become even better at arranging your time. Some tips from your colleagues follow:

✐ Always bring a geographical perspective to what you have to do. Like if you're running errands, make a map, at least in your mind, and do your run in some kind of logical order, so that you're not going back and forth. It's the same idea as when you make a shopping list and you group all your dairy together on the list and all your produce and all your meat and all your drinks so that you're not running from one aisle to the other, using up extra energy for no good reason.

✐ The Internet is the answer. It's changed my life. A lot of the shopping I used to have to run around for I can now do with a click of the mouse. I love it!

❧ I try to make the most of my commute. Since I'm in the car a lot, I do my "reading" by listening to books on tape. In fact, in recent years, it's the only way I've been able to "read." I'm also thinking about dictating notes to myself as I drive. Just sitting there looking out at traffic doesn't do it for me.

❧ I've come to realize that an important factor in my becoming more organized and finding the necessary time I need in my life is to relax my standards in certain areas. At work, I can't relax my standards. I can't serve up a dish that's less than perfect. But in the other areas of my life where I've always felt the need to be perfect, I've gotten beyond that. Like housecleaning, for instance. I used to be so compulsive about it. Now I prioritize my cleaning the way I prioritize my to-do list. I've got my daily tasks—making the bed, for instance—that have to get done. Then there are my weekly tasks, like cleaning the bathroom, and my monthly tasks, like pulling the sofa out from the wall and cleaning behind it. And then there are my yearly or more tasks, like turning the mattresses.

❧ Multitask! You hear a lot about this these days, and not everyone can do it, but you should at least give it a try. File your nails while you're on the phone. Read while you do the recumbent bike. Talk to your mother while you straighten a drawer. You'll see what a difference it makes to do this.

The concept of *mise en place* and how it relates to being organized is so important and so multifaceted that we could just keep going, if space permitted. In the next chapter, however, we extend our discussion of

Beating the Morning Madness

Mornings are hell in certain households, but they don't have to be. No matter how many of you there are to get out in the morning, it's still possible to do the drill without a lot of screaming and aggravation. Some ideas from your peers follow:

❧ Anyone and everyone living in your house should understand exactly what their morning jobs are. Teach your family to pack their school bags, briefcases, the baby's diaper bag, and whatever else is needed for the next day the night before, and put them by the door or in any other predetermined location.

❧ Lay out whatever you need to wear for the next day the night before. Uniforms need to be clean and pressed . . . but not in the morning!

❧ Keep a chalkboard, a dry-eraser board, or a pencil and pad by the door for any last-minute messages or notes.

❧ A bowl of small change goes a long way toward commutes, tolls, school lunches, newspaper money, or whatever. Empty your pockets at night, and pick up the change in the morning.

❧ Even though you're the culinary professional, if you have kids, get them into the habit of making their own lunches. It's good growth for them, but make sure they do it the night before, not in the morning.

organization to those broad strokes by which we organize our lives. In other words, we will be talking about goals—how to set them and how to realize them.

Bringing Home the Bacon

With its high fat and salt content, bacon may not be the most "politically correct" food at the moment, but it remains one of the most delicious edibles around and will certainly play a part in your cooking career, unless you find yourself in a vegetarian establishment. It's a wonderful addition to corn chowder, it pairs beautifully with liver, and it makes a savory addition to many sandwiches, not least of which are the classic club and the humble but delicious BLT. Making bacon doesn't have to be the mess you would expect it to be. In fact, bacon doesn't even have to be fried. A recipe follows for perfectly crisp bacon every time. The secret is to use the oven, not the stovetop.

- Preheat the oven to 400°.
- Arrange slices of thin- or thick-cut bacon in a jelly roll pan. Make sure slices don't overlap. Place the pan on an oven rack in the middle position.
- Roast until the fat begins to render, five to six minutes. Then rotate the pan, front to back, and continue roasting, five to six more minutes for thin-cut bacon, eight to 10 minutes for thick-cut bacon.
- Transfer carefully with tongs to a paper-towel-lined plate. Drain and serve.

Chapter 4

It's a Goal!

et's face it, you haven't chosen the easiest field in the world. If you were working as a high school teacher, a geologist employed by a state environmental agency, a nurse practitioner, and so on, the signposts on your way to success would probably be much more clearly defined, and your chances of attaining success in those fields might be a more orderly sort of business. More responsibility, yearly review, regular promotions . . . that sort of thing. But you've chosen a kind of "glamour" field where success can often prove capricious. One year you're the hot new chef in town or the caterer of choice for art openings and black-tie fund-raising affairs. The next year your cuisine has fallen out of favor, the economy is in a nosedive, and your restaurant has been undermined by personnel problems. Now you're no longer the flavor of the month. In fact, you feel like yesterday's lasagna, hanging around and waiting to be microwaved.

In a field like the culinary profession, it is important to have clear ideas about what constitutes success. It also is important that you possess good coping strategies for those inevitable times when success feels out of reach. Don't forget—your profession is marked by "hills and valleys." Everyone in your field goes through them—they are inescapable—so you have to be able to enjoy the hills and prepare for the valleys. This chapter is a good place to begin sorting out your feelings.

The Fundamentals of Success

No matter what field you're in—whether you're a movie star, a career army officer, a professional hockey player, or a pastry chef—success is a complicated and very personal matter. Some people enjoy extraordinary levels of success, and we stand in awe of them—Steven Spielberg, Wolfgang Puck, Oprah Winfrey—as successful as these folks are, however, they too have their private demons, like everyone else in the world, and, trust us, they do not *have it all*. No one does. Everyone has some area of disappointment in her or his life. It may be marital strife, money problems, health issues, conflicts with your offspring, or ethical mistakes. No one goes through life unscathed by disappointment, so we take that as a given, and we consider success within that framework.

Success does not mean the same thing to all people. There isn't just one way to be successful. Let's hear what your fellow culinary professionals have to say on this subject.

∽ It's taken me a while to figure out what success means for me in terms of the food world. You know, there are so many high rollers, and you start to feel that if you don't own your own place and you don't have a TV show and *Food & Wine* hasn't named you one of America's "top young chefs," then you're an also-ran. But that's a lot of *foie gras*, if you ask me. Success is a very personal thing. I'm feeling pretty good right now—I've got a job, I'm doing what I love, I'm supporting myself, I have a future. I don't have to see my face on a magazine cover to think that I'm a success.

∽ Some people will tell you that success is simply about making money—end of story. I don't agree. To me, there's a lot more to success than that. Are you a good human being? Do you do your job well? Do you work hard? Do people trust you, and do you trust people? Money is nice, but you know what they say—it's only money.

∽ Some people say that if you hang in there for years, and if you work hard enough and are patient enough, you'll achieve success. But the more I look around me, the more I've come to see that food is really a young person's field. I don't know any chefs who suddenly hit the big time at 55. And I don't know many people at 55 who have the stamina it takes to be successful in the food world.

꿿 I went into the culinary field as a third career. I had a managerial position with a phone company first, then I did some interior decorating, and then I realized that cooking was my true love. Although it does require some stamina, there's plenty of room in the field for the older chef. In fact, in my culinary school, I'd say the median age was early 30s. You just have to find the right situation. Maybe it would be in a health center or a retirement community. The idea of bringing really wonderful food to older people is something that should definitely be explored. There's a real need for flair and imagination to stimulate those older appetites.

꿿 To be successful in this field, you have to be ambitious. You have to curry up to people with money, first as your customers, then as your investors. If you're into food because you think it's some kind of art form, and you won't compromise yourself by putting ketchup on the steak if Mrs. Rockefeller asks for it, you really might want to think about finding another field, because chances are you ain't going to make it in this one.

꿿 When I think of success, I think of what's involved in surviving the tough times. Anybody can be a winner when things are going well—that's no challenge. It's when you're in a bad place—a kitchen where people treat you badly, for instance, or you've opened a restaurant that no one's coming to—that's when your real stuff has to come out. What's that expression? When the going gets tough, the tough get going.

꙳ My dad always says that if you want to get by in life and make a success of yourself, you need to have a sense of humor. There are too many crazy people around, and if you don't laugh at them they'll drag you down. I can't think of any field where that applies more than the one we're in. By the fifth time if you're not laughing when a customer returns the Tuna Tartare because it's "undercooked," you're going to be in big trouble.

꙳ I had this instructor in culinary school who told us that the thing about successful people is that they see the big picture. They don't let details hang them up. They identify what they want, and they go after it.

꙳ My older brother more or less raised me, and he could be some pain in the neck. He was always yelling at us that we didn't work hard enough. We were lazy, he'd say. You can't get ahead in this world unless you're willing to put in the hours. Well, you know what? Bobby was so right. One thing about this field is you can't get by without doing the work. There really are no free rides, and a big part of success has to do with just learning and practicing and working at getting good at something. For the most part, it's not about magic. In the kitchen, it's really about the hours you put in, developing your technique, experimenting, and getting really, really good at what you do.

❧ I don't know anyone who doesn't want to be successful. But the fact is that we don't all get to experience success, and even those of us who do sometimes have to wait a very long time before it comes. Having been a serious athlete when I was young, I had to figure some of this out at an early age. When I lost a game—I was a pitcher—I had to learn not to beat up on myself. You really don't help your chances of success by wearing yourself out with self-criticism. Instead, just tell yourself that everyone makes mistakes. Everyone goes through periods where they're not lucky and nothing's happening for them. Keep your good feelings about yourself alive by being good to yourself, and you'll survive until success is ready to visit you.

Success Do's and Don'ts

You all know the expression "Shooting yourself in the foot." It means finding ways to undermine your success. Why do people do this? They may have some very conflicted feelings about success. For example, in certain cultures, parents hope that their children will surpass them in terms of material success, while in other cultures to do so would be frowned upon. If you come from such a culture, you might be avoiding success for this reason. Or you might have fears of success because deep down you feel a certain sense of inadequacy that you've never dealt with, and you're afraid that if you seem to be successful, you might somehow be "exposed." It is helpful to have some sense of the ways that we can encourage success in ourselves and the ways that so many of us discourage ourselves.

Perfectionism

A number of people we spoke to cited perfectionism as one of the leading "success don'ts." Their comments follow:

✒ I look around me and I look at myself and I see that one of the big traps in this field is perfectionism. A lot of chefs, including myself, suffer from this. I mean, it's fine to want to be really, really good, but there's a difference between being good and being perfect.

✒ Perfectionism is basically a way of punishing yourself. None of us are perfect. You could be the world's best sushi chef or the greatest *saucier* in the world and still have a really bad day. When you come down to it, aiming for perfection is a truly bad idea and can only leave you with the bitter taste of disappointment. Who needs that when there are so many sweet things in the world?

✒ I have perfectionism in my genes. I grew up in a home where everything had to be perfect. Every drape had to go with every piece of upholstery, and every shoe had to match every dress, and if you had a tiny little spot on something you were wearing it was the end of the world. Now that I'm an adult, I know that perfectionism is completely counterproductive to success. Feeling like you can never achieve what you hope to achieve is the opposite of motivation, and motivation is what breeds success.

Procrastination

In as structured a field as the one you've found yourself in, procrastination may not seem like a big trap. After all, you're not going to dillydally about getting the entrees on the table. But procrastination can be a trap in terms of the way you pursue your career in the long run. Here is how your fellow culinary professionals see the issue:

❧ I've never been a great student—I'm the first to admit it. It's just not where my head goes naturally. All through high school, the operative word with me was "procrastination." If I could put something off until the next day, that's what I'd do. Better yet, the next week. Better still, forever. It's a hard habit to break. Then I found culinary school, and I thought I was over it, because I was really interested and excited about what I was doing. But I realize that I'm still struggling with my procrastination problem. Right now I'm working in a job that I really don't like, but I've been putting off looking for something else.

❧ Remember Scarlett O'Hara in *Gone with the Wind?* "I'll think about that tomorrow, at Tara." Me, if I can think of something tomorrow, that's what I'll do. Anything I don't like—doing my taxes, going to the dentist—I just put it off and put it off and get more and more guilty and more and more uptight. It's terrible.

༄ I've always had such a problem with procrastination that I actually had to get some counseling to help me deal with it, and now I know some good techniques. "Procrastination-busters," my counselor calls them. For instance, if I'm dreading something—like, let's say, I've agreed to do a food article for the local paper when I'm really not a writer—then I'll find some little bitty part of the job that I can start with. Maybe it's sharpening pencils. Maybe it's doing a little research on the Internet. Whatever it is, it has to be something so that I don't allow myself to sit there and be paralyzed.

༄ All my life my parents were on my back about how I was such a procrastinator and how they had to light a fire under me to get me to do any little thing. It was such a drag. But guess what? Now that I'm out in the world I've discovered that *everyone* procrastinates! Okay, maybe everyone doesn't procrastinate as much as I do, but it's not such a terrible sin. It's just a human quality, and you recognize it and you deal with it and you don't have to tell yourself that you're the world's worst lowlife because you do it now and then, okay?

Game Plans and Mission Statements

Some of the "success do's" that your fellow culinary professionals point out next are game plans and mission statements, which can enable you to effectively keep your eye on the prize.

༄ My dad owned a diner in New Haven and always did well with it, so I try to listen to him because he knows what he's talking about. He says that anyone who owns a business or wants to own a business needs a business plan. It's the blueprint that gets you from here to there. It tells you what you should expect to make and what you have to spend. If you don't have a business plan, no one's going to lend you a cent. My dad says that until I have my own restaurant, which is my dream, and actually have a business plan, I should think of *myself* as a business. But instead of making a business plan, I should make a game plan, and the game plan will tell me where I can expect to be in a year, in two years, in five years, maybe even in 10 years.

꿈 If you have a goal, then you need a game plan to reach that goal. Not having a game plan is like taking a car trip without a road map.

꿈 I back up my game plan with a mission statement. If you ever look at a business plan, it always includes a mission statement. The mission statement defines who you are and identifies your goals. It really helps you to see your life in such concrete terms.

꿈 Becoming a caterer was this mountain I've had to climb. Everybody always talked about what a fantastic cook I was. Every time I gave a party people couldn't stop raving, and I got so much pure satisfaction out of just feeding people. But it's a long way from feeding people to running a business. I had a lot of hurdles to get over. I'm divorced with two young children, and going to culinary school was really tough. That's why I felt it was so important to make a mission statement for myself early on. I wrote it down on a 3 × 5 index card, and I had it laminated—no kidding. I've updated my statement as I go on, and it really helps to keep me on track.

 *Goal Setting*

Success may seem like something that just "happens" or not, but in fact it comes from setting and reaching specific building blocks called "goals." Before you even get to your goals, however, you have to have *motivation*. Basically, there are two types of motivation: *extrinsic* and *intrinsic*. Extrinsic motivation can be thought of as an outside reward for what you do. Your wife offers to buy you a moped if you give up smoking—that's extrinsic. Intrinsic motivation is the motivation that comes from within you. You decide to give up smoking because you know how important it is for you to maintain good health. Intrinsic motivation usually is more long lasting and effective than the extrinsic variety.

Once you have an understanding of motivation, you can begin to focus on the business of setting goals. Let's hear what your fellow professionals have to say on that topic.

✍ There are goals and then there are goals. In other words, some of your goals are going to be short term—you can achieve them tomorrow or next week or a couple of months down the road. Taking a vacation to Bermuda might be considered a short-term goal (depending on how long it takes you to pull together the vacation money). Owning your own restaurant is the long-term goal for so many of us in this field, and that can take years to realize.

❧ When I think of long-term goals, they're not so much about *things* as they are about *feelings*. For instance, one of my long-term goals is to feel financially independent and secure. Then I have a goal to be in a long-term relationship with someone I love and to have children. When I really think about what my goals are, one is them is definitely to feel really good about myself. Now some of these goals may take a very long time to achieve, even a lifetime, but hey—that's life.

❧ Setting goals is a great idea, but like most other things in life, there's a right way to go about it and a wrong way. The wrong way is to set goals for yourself where you're continually falling short of them. That's going to leave you feeling disappointed and even discouraged, which is counter to the whole idea of goal setting.

❧ My long-term goal is to open up a little restaurant on the coast of Maine. I don't know whether I'll ever really be able to accomplish that, but I also know that I don't want to worry about it all the time and feel like I'm always falling short. So what I've learned to do is to break down my goals into smaller "goal units" that I feel confident I can accomplish. So an example of a goal unit that I've accomplished toward my long-term goal was taking a business course so that if I ever do own a restaurant, I'll have some idea of what I'm doing. Saving money every month toward my long-term goal is another example of a goal unit. Sometimes I don't even accomplish my goal unit—my car, for example, might need a new alternator, and there goes my savings that month—but it's not the end of the world.

❧ Setting goals is fine, but they have to be thought out. You can't just say, "I'm going to do so-and-so." You need to figure out exactly what you have to do in order to get so-and-so done. You've got to ask yourself questions like: "What skills do I need to reach my goal?" "Do I need to take more classes?" "Can I find an advisor or a mentor to help me?"

❧ Goals and dreams are two different things. I once had a dream to be a ballet dancer. I broke both my legs in an automobile accident. End of dream. Goals should be something that it's possible for you to achieve. If you've got chronic back problems, for instance, don't go into the restaurant business. That's a no-brainer.

❧ Goal setting never ends. It's not as if you get to the top of the heap and then you're finished—no more goals. Just look at any amazingly successful person, and you'll see that they're always raising the bar higher.

❧ You stand a much better chance of achieving your goals if you frame them in positive language. Positive language goes such a long way toward breeding good feelings. In other words, writing down your goals should not become an occasion for you to dump on yourself. Instead of writing "I'm not going to cheat on another diet," try instead for "I'm going to achieve my desired weight." See the difference?

✎ One thing that's really important about goals is to make sure that they're *your* goals. Don't worry about other people's goals. My parents wanted me to be a doctor. I wanted to be a chef. It took a lot of discussion, but I won. Which was a lucky thing for mankind, because I would have been a terrible doctor.

Dealing with Disappointment

Goals are important, but just as important is the way you cope with not meeting them. Your capacity to deal with disappointment will prove key to how successful you are at getting through life. Let's hear what your fellow culinary professionals have to say on this subject:

✎ Life is full of land mines. Like one Christmas I was working at this restaurant in downtown New York, and I got fired. My boss felt really bad about it, but it couldn't be helped—it was post–September 11, he was struggling to hang on, and he had to cut payroll. Well, I went out for the obligatory getting drunk after work bit, but in the middle of my third Black Russian, I just got a hold of myself. I thought of all those people who had been lost in the World Trade Center, and I said, "You're crying about *this*? Shame on you." The real lesson was that whatever happens to you, something worse is happening to someone else.

If you fall short of a goal you've set for yourself, just move on. That's life.

🍥 Disappointments can lead you down streets you wouldn't find yourself on otherwise. It's like the Buddhist thing of "what's the gift?" I lost my job a couple of years ago in this restaurant I'd been working in. The owner had a massive heart attack and couldn't keep it up. I was pretty crazed for a while, but I wound up starting a meat-pie business with a friend of mine. We've worked our buns off and haven't made a lot of money, but we're still alive, and it's been a great growth experience. That's the gift.

🍥 My parents always taught us that if we've been disappointed in something, it's important to look at the situation and to see what you did right and what you did wrong. Everything is a learning experience, they always told us. There's no such thing as failure. There's just good stuff and bad stuff, and you've got to learn from it all.

Striking the Right Balance

As a culinary professional, you are clearly familiar with the idea of "balance" in a dish. Too sweet . . . too savory . . . too much salt . . . too little pepper. It's all a matter of tasting and testing until you find what's right. Similarly, it's important to strike the right balance when it comes to your goals. Too much or too little emphasis on your goals will produce an unsatisfying result. Your fellow professionals said the following on this subject:

❧ I try to pace myself. When I was starting out, all I did was work, work, work. I didn't have a life. Now that I've reached a certain plateau—I'm an executive chef—I've decided to go a little easier on myself. I'm not into the whole macho work thing as much anymore. I make sure I get my downtime when I can go out with my watercolors and enjoy nature or just lie back and listen to Bach. It's a whole new me.

❧ I raise the bar high. That's the way I was brought up, and that's what I believe in. I make a point of continually trying to better myself. I never stop learning new things. I teach, I write, I travel—all in addition to holding down my job as a *sous chef* in one of the capital's best restaurants. I see myself as a work in progress, and I refuse to tread water, even for a minute.

❧ I've owned my own restaurant for the last six years and I love it, but there's a real danger in owning your own place. You start seeing yourself as a money machine. The more hours you put in, the more money you can make. It's not so healthy.

❧ I just quit a job being the right-hand person to this woman who has this huge catering business. She's a really bright, talented, dynamic individual, but she's a total workaholic. You know, the word "workaholic" has become a kind of macho compliment in our culture, but in fact when you work with a workaholic, you come to realize how screwed up it is. Generally, they don't really get any more done than normal people. A lot of them are just sort of obsessive-compulsive personalities who take more time doing simple or even unnecessary tasks just so they can say they're working. Work is their drug of choice, and like any drug, it can be badly abused. Plus, most workaholics expect the people they work with to be workaholics. They don't understand that some of us want a life.

✥ I have the tendency to be a workaholic, and I've really had to be conscious of it and fight against it. One thing I do is I take two vacations a year, no matter what. Sometimes I'll stay at home, but I don't clean out closets or paint the back room. I do special things that my crazy schedule down at the restaurant doesn't usually permit. I'll go to a French film in the afternoon. I'll sit for an hour in the museum staring at a Rodin. I'll go smell the flowers in the park. Some of my best vacations have been spent at home.

✥ If you tend to be a workaholic like I am, you have to alert the people in your life to the fact, and you have to ask them to let you know when you're off in your orbit. My daughter's really good about it. She's only 10, but she knows enough to pull me out of the kitchen and say, "Ma. Enough already."

✥ One of the things that gives me balance is that I don't just live in the world of food. My closest friends are mostly from college. One's a pediatric nurse, one's a painter, one's a criminal lawyer, and we get together a lot. That means that I don't live, eat, and breathe restaurant talk, like a lot of chefs I know.

As you can tell from this chapter, setting goals can be a complicated business, underscored by complicated feelings about success. Another area of your life as a culinary professional that is just as complicated involves your relationships with fellow professionals in the workplace. We explore this important subject in the next chapter.

More Mashed Potatoes, Please

The stock market has crashed. The home team has lost the World Series. It's snowing in April. Quick—how are you going to comfort your customers? The answer is easy—mashed potatoes! Mashed potatoes are the last word in comfort foods, and making them is not a mystery. You do have to know what you're doing, however. Follow these steps:

- Start with waxy potatoes. Starchy potatoes won't work.
- Wash and peel the potatoes. Cut each one into four to six pieces in roughly uniform size.
- Place the potatoes in a pot, and cover them with water, to which you have added a tablespoon of salt. Bring to a boil, reduce to a simmer, and cook until the potatoes are tender. Do not overcook.
- When the potatoes are cooked, drain them in a colander. Make sure that they are very dry before proceeding. Transfer the dry potatoes to the bowl of an electric mixer. Using your whip attachment,

whip the potatoes for 30 to 45 seconds. Scrape down the sides and bottom of the bowl, and whip for another 15 seconds or until the potatoes are smooth and without lumps.

- For five pounds of potatoes, add four ounces of melted butter and eight fluid ounces of hot milk. Whip on the lowest speed until all of the ingredients are incorporated and the potatoes have the consistency you are looking for.

Many diners feel that mashed potatoes don't need any more seasoning than salt and perhaps a grinding of white pepper, but garlic mashed potatoes have become quite popular on today's menus. Horseradish, shallots, and wasabi are other flavoring alternatives to try.

Chapter 5

Too Many Cooks

ew situations in the world feel more hierarchical than a restaurant kitchen. Everybody
has an appointed place; everybody has an
appointed job; and it seems at times as though everyone has a big ego. People can develop a very emotional
and proprietary attitude around the foods they prepare,
and a competitive atmosphere can soon arise in the
kitchen that can veer out of control unless the players
feel like they are on a team that really knows how to
work together. Throw into the mix a good deal of heat,
a substantial level of noise, and all of the other ingredients of a high-stress setting, and you don't need us to
tell you how pressing the issue of getting along with
others can become. This chapter offers strategies from
your fellow professionals for everything from conflict

resolution to anger management to gender bias and issues of diversity. Working with subordinates and apprentices also will be discussed. So without further ado, let us begin.

Developing a Base of Good Communications

You all know what a base is. It is the foundation for a soup. A broth, made either from meat, poultry, fish, or vegetables, is the kind of base most often used to start a soup, and then, of course, we add all of our other ingredients. Similarly, when we talk about team playing, we start with the "base" of communications. There can be no team playing, as there can be no delicious soup, without that strong and sturdy base. If you cannot make your wants and needs known, and if you can't hear the wants and needs of other people, then you're bound to have a difficult time being part of the team. Your culinary colleagues had a lot to say on this topic:

✐ Too many of us think of communication only as spoken language. It's just not so. *Everything* is communication. The hand signals we give each other. The expressions on our face. Our body language. In fact, a lot of unspoken communication is even more immediate and emphatic than our spoken communication. If you really want to be able to work well with other people, you have to be able to read those nonverbal cues, because a lot of times they telegraph just as fast, if not faster, than words do.

❧ Body language speaks just as loudly as spoken language does. The problem is that a lot of times you don't know you're speaking in body language. You might think you're not saying anything, but the way you cock your head or fold your arms can speak volumes of disapproval. Better make sure you know what your body is saying, because you can really ruin somebody's day without even opening your mouth.

❧ I work with a chef who's basically a good guy, but he stands over me whenever we're talking. I mean, he's literally right in my face. But he doesn't seem to understand the whole concept of space barriers and personal space. I remember that I once read something about how it's okay for your family, your close friends, and your lovers to stand a foot away from you when they're talking, but everybody else has to back up to four to 12 feet. Including your boss!

❧ I know that a lot of people think it's wrong to judge someone on some superficial thing, like the color of that person's eyes or whether he's tall or short or fat or thin, and I totally agree . . . except for when it comes to a person's voice. I had to hire a cook for our staff, and I had it down to two very qualified people. They were both out of cooking schools and came with great references and all. On paper, they looked like equal matches. But one of them, when she opened her mouth, it was like chalk scraping on a blackboard. Or like Marge Simpson yelling at Homer. I couldn't deal with listening to that all the time, so I gave the job to the other person. I wanted to tell that woman that she needed to work on her voice, to make it softer and less strident, but I couldn't bring myself to do it. I hope someone will.

ᕫ I've got a young guy working on my staff who's just brilliant with food. He has this remarkable creativity that never sails over the top, you know? But the problem with him is that he's a bad listener. I'll tell him something, and it goes in one ear and out the other. It finally dawned on me that maybe he has a hearing loss. He played in a rock band before he got into food—that could do it. So I directed his attention to the problem, suggested that he go for a hearing assessment, and, sure enough, he has a deficit.

ᕫ I know that people come in all different packages, and I'm pretty tolerant of a lot of different personal styles, but I have to confess that I've had a few silent souls on staff, and that's been a problem for me. They were good workers, but they never asked questions. To me, a big part of good communication is the give and take of questions and answers. I like people who work for me to act like they're engaged and interested, and nothing spells that out more than asking good questions.

ᕫ In our kitchen, we have a policy of "communication equality." That means that everyone gets to say what he or she wants to say. We don't have to follow a chain of command around speaking. If you've got a question, or if something's bothering you, spit it out!

❧ Here's a good idea: when you're trying to communicate with someone, ask yourself if you've picked a good time. I've had people come over to me when I'm turning a turkey to ask for a raise. Hey, pal, I want to say—I can't turn a turkey and listen to you at the same time, okay?

❧ When I first started working in the restaurant business, I had a problem. I'd be in the kitchen and somebody would be trying to talk to me, and I couldn't filter out all the noises and distractions so that I could pay attention to what the person was trying to say. I suffer from "selective attention"—when I go to a party, I can't stop looking all around me, even when somebody's trying to talk to me—and the hectic environment of the kitchen was tough.

❧ The listening end of communication is just as important as the speaking end. Both parties have to hold up their ends of the bargain. If I'm speaking, I have to try not to bore the other person or take up too much of his or her time. If I'm listening, and the other person is boring me or taking up too much of *my* time, I have to somehow convey that. One of the other station chefs in our kitchen is a nice guy, but he'll talk your ear off. I'll just clear my throat, and then I'll try folding my arms, and if that doesn't work, I'll say "Excuse me" or "Bad time, Jack." What else are you going to do?

❧ I've been in my first job as a chef for the last year, and the man who owns the restaurant is a really rotten communicator. He'll tell me one thing and then act like he's told me something else altogether different. It's created a lot of stress for me, but my sister-in-law, who's a psychologist, gave me this good technique to use with him. It's called "reflective listening." Let's say he tells me to put a second vegetarian entrée on the menu, because he's decided that the area we live in has a lot of vegetarians, and he wants to give them a choice. So I'll say to him, "Okay, Frank—we're going to put a second vegetarian entrée on the menu." When he hears his words coming back to him—*reflected*, as it were—he might abandon the plan right away, or he might confirm it. Either way, it helps to establish what exactly is going on.

 *Personality and Attitude*

We talked about communication as a "base," but we could argue as well that your personality and attitude also are vital ingredients in that base. Working in the culinary profession makes a lot of demands on you, and your personality and attitude are likely to determine how well you can meet those demands. As you know, the food world is a highly competitive and stressful arena. There is a shared goal—selling food to customers—but then again there also is a high degree of individualism built into the business. Most cooks want to evolve into chefs, and chefs often have the personalities of orchestra conductors. They like things done their way, and they view themselves, often rightly so, as highly creative individuals. So the combination of the individualistic orientation and the team ethos that must exist in any good kitchen can sometimes be hard to sort out. Let's hear what your fellow professionals have to say on the subject of personality and attitude.

✍ I think basically I'm kind of a shy, introverted person, but I've had to learn how to be otherwise to survive in Chef Rudy's kitchen. It's [a] pretty wild and woolly atmosphere, with everybody grabbing everything off the shelves, and if you're not a grabber—or feel that you can't *learn* to become a grabber—there's a good chance that you'll get lost in the shuffle.

✍ I'm a middle sister. Never felt I had enough attention, always feeling like I'm not "getting." But at least if I know what my problem is, I can do something about it. Stop whining, for one thing. I used to be such a whiner—it drove the rest of my family crazy. I think I even got fired from my first job for whining, although of course nobody told me that in so many words. I'm smart enough, however, to have gotten some perspective on myself—nothing that a few years in therapy couldn't achieve—and now I never whine. Never, ever. I ask for what I want instead of complaining about what I don't get.

✍ To survive in this world—and I don't just mean the world of food, I mean the world at large—you have to learn how to become an assertive person. Now keep in mind that there's a big difference between being assertive and aggressive. I know from aggressive, believe me—some of my worst boyfriends were real aggressive creeps. Being assertive, however, means standing up for yourself and being able to verbalize what you need and want. Being assertive means operating in a way that's clear, uncharged, and productive.

↝ A lot of the women in my family tend to be victims. I always worried that I would inherit that gene, and to some extent I think I have. I started off in this field working for this chef who used to give me nightmares. He would scream at me—and I mean scream—in front of the whole staff about how clumsy I was. Can you imagine? I cried a lot that year, but another one of the station chefs helped me out. He was a really sweet man who took it upon himself to teach me the secret of assertiveness. He told me that assertiveness is a three-step process. You begin with *I feel*. You go on to *I want*. You end with *I will*. So, in my case, I said, "I *feel* like I'm being used as a punching bag." Next it was, "I *want* to be treated with basic minimal respect." Ending with, "I *will* make it known that I expect nothing less." Well, I made it known, and I was fired, but at least I retained some self-respect and learned the trick of assertiveness for future purposes.

↝ I've suffered over the years from depression. It's a real factor in my personality, and I have to take it into account. I'm on antidepressants, and that's been good and certainly represents a direction that anyone should explore with a physician if you think it's necessary, but another useful thing I've learned to do on my own is called "reframing." Reframing basically is an adaptation that allows you to change the meaning of an event.

For instance, if my boss tells me that "business is bad," my personality—gloomy Gus that I am—might immediately lead me to think that I'm going to get the ax. Then I step back and I start reframing. My boss and I get along great. I've been working for him for eight years with no problems. I tell myself, "If business is bad, we have to figure out how to make it better. Maybe a Cajun night. Maybe a seafood night." Whatever the answer is, if I reframe, then I stay away from that dark place I really don't need to venture into.

❧ In the culinary world, you've got to roll with the punches. Everything happens fast, fast, fast. You know the way you can throw butter in a hot pan and it'll flame up? That's, like, a metaphor for what happens to all of us in the kitchen at some time or another. We have our little disasters, we get frazzled, we yell at our coworkers to blow off the steam. If some poor little lamb gets caught in the crossfire, he or she is just going to have to learn to suck it up and continue on his or her merry way, because this stuff will happen, there's no way around it, and you don't have to make a tragedy out of every cross word somebody says to you.

❧ One of my good friends at work is also a station chef, like me. She's great, but she's into everybody's business. That's just the way she is. I try to warn her. I say, "Sally, be careful. We spend all day working with these people every day. It's like a family. If you make one mistake, if you betray one confidence, you're going to pay for it." Believe me, it's better to keep a low profile and not try to get next to everybody.

❧ I remember the first time I went to work in a restaurant. It was run by a husband and wife, and their son and daughter were involved and some cousins and whatnot. Well, one day, there was such a blowout in the kitchen you'd have thought it was World War III. I guess I looked kind of upset, because one of the cousins came over to me and said, "What can I tell you? It's a family business." The point of the story is that blowups happen in the restaurant business. Your best bet is to keep your nose clean, and always try to be neutral.

❧ Some people just have super-competitive personalities. I don't think it makes life easy. I try to share whatever I know with everyone else. I think of myself as being part of a team, which means that sometimes I help somebody out, and other times other people help me out. I like it that way.

❧ Always be generous with your knowledge. My Great-Aunt Lydia made the world's best lasagna, but she would never share the recipe with anyone. When she died, the lasagna recipe went to the grave with her. No more Lydia, no more lasagna. End of story.

 ## Conflict Resolution

No matter how excellent your communications skills are or how sunny and even tempered your personality may be, there will inevitably come a time when you find yourself at odds with your coworkers. Such a situation can be aggravating, but hopefully the distress will prove short term. One way to try to ensure that it remains short term is to become adept at *conflict resolution*. Without conflict resolution—which we can define as the means by which to negotiate differences and come to some form of mutual agreement—the tensions and bad feelings that can develop around conflict may linger for the long term and may even fester to produce deeper conflict.

Here's how some of your colleagues mend fences.

✑ Wow, big topic. I guess the place to start is with yourself. You can have all the techniques in the world for dealing with conflict, but if you're not really in touch with who *you* are, then it's not going to count for much. By this I mean that you have to assess what kind of person you are and what you're bringing to the party. Are you petty? Narcissistic? Are you hypersensitive? Are you willing to meet people part way, or do you dig in your heels? Take an inventory of your personal characteristics—maybe you'll want to solicit some input on the subject from family and friends you trust—and then start working on the things that you think need changing.

✑ Conflict resolution will only really work in an atmosphere of trust. If you're operating in a kitchen where all those knives are making you uncomfortable because you never know who's going to stab you in the back, then it's unlikely that you're going to have a whole lot of effective conflict resolution.

❧ One of the things you have to keep in mind when you're working at conflict resolution is the anger styles of the people you're dealing with. A lot of that has to do with personality, and some of it has to do with the family culture that these individuals come out of. I have a friend at work, for instance, who grew up in this family where no one ever expressed anger. They smiled when they were upset about things. So Sandy has this very passive-aggressive personality. Now we have another guy in the kitchen, Olivier, who's a real road-rage kind of guy. I've had problems with both of them at some time or another—hey, when you work in a kitchen everyone seems to have problems with each other at some time or another—and I have to use different conflict resolutions with them.

❧ For me, the key to conflict resolution is the ability to listen, and I guess that hearkens back to the issue of communication skills. But so many people just raise their voices in a conflict and never step back to hear what the other person has to say. Hearing it doesn't mean you have to buy it, but at least try to engage in a dialogue.

❧ Conflict resolution is like a dance. One person steps forward, another person steps back, then reverse. You know what I mean? Sometimes you're dealing with people who just don't want to give an inch, and that's frustrating.

❧ Always remember that the person you're trying to resolve with *is* a person. I do this little trick to remind myself of that fact. I always use the name of the other person—a lot. I'll say, "John, you seem upset about something." Or, "Mary, why don't you tell me what's bothering you?" I also think that when the other person hears his or her name, it softens the anger.

❧ If you want to get beyond the conflict, you must always stay in the present. Don't go back to the past to rehash a bunch of old transgressions. Don't start saying, "And then, Pierre, there was the time you slammed the oven door and totaled my Grand Marnier soufflé!" The soufflé is a done deed—no need to bring it up now when what you're really arguing about is the fact that he still hasn't paid you back that $50 you lent him.

❧ Before, after, and, if possible, during a conflict, I'll try to share a good feeling with the other person. I'll figure out something good to say about him or her, even if it kills me. That way, I can acknowledge that there's a problem, but I put the problem in the context of something bigger. For example, I might say something like, "Jean, you always say what's on your mind, and I admire you for that. But I'm not sure you understood me correctly, blah blah blah." Works like a charm.

❧ Wolves do this thing when they get into a fight: one of them makes itself submissive and shows its jugular to its enemy. This display usually puts a stop to the fighting. I learn from wolves. When I'm in a fight, I'll say something to the other person like, "You know, I really feel I could use your help to figure a way out of this mess." When I do this, the other person usually rushes to help me, and I never feel like I've lost face.

Quite the opposite. I feel like I've figured out a way to manage the situation.

〜 My friend Paul works in a kitchen in Chicago. It's a very upscale operation, and he loves it, but recently he had this huge blowout with this woman who works in the front. Some nonsense about some friend of Paul's who had called for a reservation and then never showed up, and the woman was just dumping on Paul, and they got into a shouting match. Paul called me, incredibly upset, he was never going to talk to that woman again, how dare she, yadda yadda. I said to him, "Paul, send her a dozen roses." "What!" he said. "And admit I was wrong?" I told him it wasn't anything of the sort. "What you'll discover," I said, "is that everybody who works with you will respect you for putting an end to this tension." Well, after some more back and forth, he did the roses bit, and it worked like magic. He was so grateful to me for giving him that idea.

〜 If you ask me, the key to resolving conflict is having a commitment to resolving conflict. If you tell yourself—and the other person—that you *will* get beyond this, then you've got a chance.

 *Anger Management*

As we've said, a restaurant kitchen can be a pretty explosive environment. Flash fires are apt to break out all over the place in such a high-stress atmosphere. If you're able to keep your anger under control, you will have much less need for conflict resolution in the first place. Here's how your colleagues handle anger:

❧ Anger is not something you have to be afraid of. It's just a normal part of life—in fact, being afraid of it can be exactly the thing that sends it out of control. You want to be familiar enough with your anger and comfortable enough to be able to take your "anger temperature." Ask yourself: How angry am I? On a scale of 1 to 10, am I a four? A seven? Am I off the charts at 11? If the answer to that last question is "yes," then you're going to have to be able to take emergency action to make sure that you're not going to do something you regret, like play bumper cars in the parking lot. Some actions, once they've been taken, cannot be undone, and the consequences can be life changing, both for you and for the object of your anger.

❧ You know that expression "an ounce of prevention is worth a pound of cure"? It makes sense when you think of it in terms of anger. I try to prevent fights by avoiding those things that I know are going to set me off. Like I always used to have a fight with my boyfriend when we'd play Ping-Pong because he's so incredibly competitive and such a sore sport if he loses. So now I don't play Ping-Pong with him anymore. If I want to do something with him, I'll suggest we watch something on TV or whatever. Something where winning doesn't come into play.

❧ If I'm really in [a] rage over something, what I'll try to do is to make myself breathe deeply. Putting oxygen into your body is definitely the right direction to go in, but you've got to make sure that you're doing *deep* breathing. That means breathing with your diaphragm, bringing it up from your gut. Shallow breathing isn't going to help anything.

✐ I try to stay away from certain "hot-button" words like "never" or "always." Those are the kinds of very charged words—"You *never* do anything right"; "I'm *always* waiting for you"—that only make things worse.

✐ Counting to 10 is one of the most brilliant pieces of advice that anybody ever came up with. It really is—I'm not kidding. Just to give you that moment of reflection, because once you say something, it's said, and it's out there, and you can't take it back. This holds particularly true for e-mail. A lot of people these days will rush to their e-mail when they're upset and unleash a torrent of fiery words, which then becomes a historical record that will follow you around forever. Don't do it!

✐ Break the chain of anger any way you can. Go out for a coffee. Brew yourself a cup of lapsang souchong. Go to the park, and take a ride on the carousel. Duck into a movie. Do whatever you have to do to divert yourself from this fury that is eating you alive.

✐ You haven't come this far in life without hearing the expression "Turn the other cheek." It's an oldie but a goodie. You really don't have to get engaged in every aggressive impulse that comes your way. Sometimes people are having a bad day, and they may snap at you. Sometimes people may be angry with someone else, and if you're there, you get caught in the crossfire. Don't get sucked into other people's anger if you can help it.

And, believe me, there's nothing wimpy about not taking the bait every time it's dangled in front of you.

🌱 Laughter is magic. I don't mean laughing in the other person's face. I mean distracting yourself from your anger with something that makes you feel good. If you're steaming, log on to "The Onion" on the Net—it's one of the funniest things going—or head home to curl up with a video of the Stooges. *Nyuk Nyuk Nyuk*. They'll make your anger go away . . . at least for awhile.

Feedback and Criticism

Sometimes conflict emanates out of criticism. After all, hearing the truth about oneself can hurt. But criticism is a vital part of the workplace, and once you get beyond the hurt, you can use this input to make important changes. Let's see what others in the field have to say about criticism:

🌱 Part of having a positive attitude is being able to handle criticism. My father was always very critical of me, so criticism was something I saw as a very negative thing, and I've had to work really hard to get better at accepting it. I used to withdraw or rationalize or try to blame other people whenever I was criticized, but now I've come to learn that the best way to handle criticism is to see it as a positive thing. It's feedback that can teach you how to become better at what you're trying to do.

🌱 I have a young woman working for me who's just an extremely defensive sort of person. God forbid I should say to her, "Laura, the curry was a little salty tonight." She'll launch into some whole routine about how the eggplant soaks up the salt so if you don't put enough in, you won't taste it, and yadda-yadda. All I want her to do is listen to me. I mean, it's my job to give her feedback. She's a talented cook, and I'd hate to lose her, but I'm starting to think that she's not worth the trouble.

✌ If you want to be part of a team, you have to learn how to receive criticism. And how to give it. Some people have such sensitive skin that if you look at them the wrong way, they fold. That's not going to cut the mustard in this business. You've got to hear what you're doing wrong, change it, and move on.

✌ I don't have an easy personality. I started hearing that from my parents when I learned to walk. No, seriously, I'm a pretty intense, demanding person, and I can be tough on my staff, but I also think I'm fair. I've had to learn a lot. Earlier on, when I too was just starting out and working in my first job as a chef, I used to lose it with some of my people. And I would say things to them that I can't believe I ever said. Stuff like, "You know, you're not very smart." Well, the person I said this to *wasn't* very smart, but there was nothing he could do about it, was there? Now if I have to criticize someone, I make sure never to get personal. I'll say things like, "It's important for you to hear me so that we can be on the same page." There's no point in attacking somebody for something that can't be changed.

✌ I work as *sous chef* for a chef who's quite brilliant but who has terrible people skills. He'll scream things at people like, "Look how sloppy you are!" Okay, maybe these people *are* a little sloppy, but that kind of treatment isn't going to get anybody anywhere. So I try to model for him. I speak to our staff the way I speak to my children, always trying to use the "I" word, not the "You" word. So instead of saying, "You're so sloppy," I'll say something like, "I would appreciate it if you could be more careful where you leave your things." I think that Luis, the chef, is finally starting to get the point.

≫ I always go for the "second opinion." For instance, if my boss says to me, "You're disorganized," I'll take a survey of my friends and family. "Hey now, listen up," I'll say. "Am I disorganized? Have you noticed this about me? Just how disorganized would you say I am?" It's a reality test, and even if it hurts, it's important to do it.

≫ Giving negative feedback can be just as hard as getting it. At first, when I found myself in the position of managing other people, I was very reluctant to criticize anyone. It just didn't feel like a part of my nature. But then I realized that I was doing my staff a disfavor by *not* criticizing them. They had to learn, after all, and if I was just going to nod and smile at everything they ever did, the learning was never going to happen.

Interfacing with the Front of the Room

Traditionally, a restaurant has always had a "back of the house"—the kitchen staff—and a "front of the house"—the service. Sometimes, the back of the house is referred to as "the heart of the house" . . . which certainly doesn't get the front of the house to feel any more fondly toward the cooks. Tension between the two worlds can be severe in certain situations. Some of your fellow culinary professionals have bridged the void in the following ways:

✎ The greatest boon to amicability between the two worlds is the advent of the open kitchen. That prevents doors from being slammed and we cooks from simmering in our orbit.

✎ It's important for the back of the house to keep in mind that the meals for the staff not be just a bunch of unattractive leftovers. As cooks, we should plan to use our skills to make people happy with glorious food . . . and that applies to waitstaff as well.

✎ Let's call a spade a spade: cooks get jealous of the gratuities that the waitstaff pulls in.

✎ I resent it when the waiters don't know anything about food. I mean, they're in the business. They need to educate themselves.

✎ In our restaurant, we've used cross-training very successfully. The servers learn basic procedures and timing in the kitchen by doing a stint on line or at the cold station. The line cook, in turn, runs food or greets the guests in the dining room. It's terrific!

✎ I've heard of restaurants where, once a week, the servers allot a percentage of their tips for the kitchen staff. I've also heard of restaurants where the kitchen staff has shared the wine and food promotions with the servers.

✐ We do a lot of team building in our restaurant. We have parties, we go on "field trips" to vineyards and farms. It makes such a difference.

Problems with Customers

As we've said elsewhere, "no" is one of the most important words to master if you're in the restaurant business. Saying no to customers can be one of the hardest things to learn how to do, but learn it you must.

A chef or a chef/owner's relationship with his or her customers is very complicated. Sometimes the customer will become a close friend. He or she has been with you from the start, loves the way you cook, and is patient when you mess up. Customers challenge you; you challenge them. You grow together.

Other times, your relationships with your customers come with loads of strings attached. They'll love you if: (1) your prices are good; (2) you've got a kids' menu; (3) you serve yak cheese or fresh Chinese gooseberries; (4) you let them design your advertising campaign; (5) you permit them to smoke; (6) you let them back you in a franchise operation. The list can go on and on. What to do? Some comments from professionals follow:

෯ I had a customer who came in three times a week. He was very important to me. He was a mainstay and part of my history. But it got to the point where he started to act like he owned the place. He brought in a case of cabernet and insisted that I try it as the house wine. Then he brought in a duck that he shot and asked me to fix it for him. What was this? His mother's kitchen or something? I had to set him straight . . . and then, sure enough, he went on to his next patsy.

෯ Someone once told me that there's a formula for customers. Forty percent will be your loyal friends; forty percent will be acquaintances that come and go; and 20 percent will show up once and never reappear. In my experience, that's been right on target.

෯ I've had to "fire" customers. I had a guy who was so loud it made dining a nightmare for everybody else. I told him he couldn't come back. It was tough, but I did it.

Gender Issues

The culinary profession has traditionally and famously been an old boys' club, with women on the outside peering in. Certainly in recent decades this unfairness has been ameliorated by great women chefs such as Julia Child and Alice Waters. In fact, in a 1992 poll,

60 percent of employees in the restaurant industry were women, and almost 30 percent of all cooking school students were women. But gender issues still loom large in the world of food, both for women chefs who have to preside over male employees and for women who are presided over by men.

Women in Power

If you were lucky enough to catch the German comedy *Mostly Martha*, then you saw an engaging portrait of a woman chef who was fanatically compulsive and in need of being thawed by a life-loving Italian male chef. Delightful as the film was, it reinforced some stereotypes about women in power. Even today, with almost four decades' worth of women's rights to look back on, the issue of assuming power continues to be a thorny one for many women. Let's see how some of our female chefs have dealt with this issue.

∿ I've had to make myself go for the spotlight. It's not in my nature and not intrinsically in the nature of most women I know. I think women tend to be recessive about grabbing attention. You remember back to middle school, how the boys were always the ones getting called on? But I'm a top chef, so I figured it was time to start acting like one. I command respect for my talents, and now, when that respect comes my way, I've learned to appreciate it and use it.

∿ You've got to get out of your comfort zone if you want to really make it as a woman in a man's world.

You've got to stretch yourself, extend yourself, test yourself. Women are too often content with hanging back and hiding their light under a bushel.

❧ I have to confess: I'm so much of a woman when it deals with power issues. I like to be liked. I *need* to be liked. And I realize I have to work against that now. I've got a bunch of men working under me, and I can't always be liked.

❧ Like most women, I tend to focus on the personal needs of everyone around me. Oh, you've got a young child at home. Oh, you're having marital problems. Oh, you never grew up. But running a kitchen is not about personal needs. It's about *business* needs. We have to turn out meals that are good enough to convince people to come back to us again. That's what it's all about, and it's ridiculous to act otherwise.

❧ Being in power means having full accountability. It's the whole "buck stops here" bit. You're assuming the responsibility, which is a big deal, and that gives you the right to say, "Okay, guys. I will listen to what you have to say, but I've got to tell you that I'm the boss, and I've got to be the one who ultimately makes the decisions."

❧ Men have an advantage because they get to practice getting along with each other in that locker room setting. They know how to crack jokes and snap towels. Women tend to get very serious and lose the fun part of it. We've got to learn to laugh and not be so defensive.

A lot of women need flexible hours for obvious reasons—children, family. The restaurant business does not lend itself well to flexible hours. Quite a few women go into the baking area because they can come in earlier and leave earlier, and their hours are somewhat more predictable than those of the line cooks.

Sexual Harassment

When women and men are thrown together in close quarters, such as in a restaurant kitchen, things happen that shouldn't. One of those "things" is sexual harassment. How do your colleagues in the field handle this issue? Let's find out:

What constitutes sexual harassment? It's when remarks are made that make you feel uncomfortable. Now you'll hear people say, "Oh, so that means your boss can't tell you that you're wearing nice earrings?" And that's entirely right, because if the subtext of his remark is something that makes you uncomfortable, you don't have to stand for it. Nothing about your hair, your clothes, your shoes, your fingernails is anybody's business but your own.

Don't kid yourself—the harassment is not going to get any better. If it's already started, it's just going to get worse. "Good morning. What a pretty blouse" is going to turn into "You're driving me crazy in that blouse." You've got to nip it in the bud, even if it's going to be hard for you to do that.

✐ Your harasser is not going to stop on his own. He's going to stop when you stand up to him and firmly tell him that you don't want any discussion of that sort again—*ever*.

✐ Don't put yourself in a vulnerable position vis-à-vis anyone who you think might take advantage of you. That means you should make a point of always having other people around. Don't go out to lunch, just the two of you. Don't come in early or stay late if that means you're going to be alone with him.

✐ Being harassed is very upsetting. Confide in other people. It helps, and you might find out that you're not the only one being hit on.

✐ Obviously, report any harassment to your supervisor. If your supervisor *is* the harasser, and there's nowhere higher to go, talk to an attorney.

✐ Don't put up with it. It's only a job. There are other jobs out there. Don't let yourself become a victim!

The Diverse Workplace

More than most situations, the culinary field is truly diverse. Not only do you have all of the diversity of ethnicity and religious and sexual choice that would characterize any workplace in the twenty-first century, but you also will find a remarkable level of internationality. If you're working in a big city, then you might expect to find staff members from the European Union, from Asia, from South and Central America, and from Africa. All of this diversity can be enormously exciting, but it also can, at times, be a challenge to navigate. Some points from professionals follow:

✐ First of all, you have to understand that your culture isn't the only culture. That's called "ethnocentricity." It's entirely possible that those traits that are valued in your culture—like extreme punctuality, for instance—may be of less importance in other cultures. There isn't one "right" way to do something. There are many ways to do something.

✐ When I hire someone for my staff, I want to make sure that they're the kind of person who can walk in somebody else's shoes. They need to have a certain level of maturity, so that they're not making inappropriate jokes or comments, which will leave me with a mess to clean up afterwards.

✐ Don't make assumptions about people based on their cultural heritage. Not all Italians are "fun loving," not all Scotsmen are "tight fisted," not all Mexicans are "lazy." But all people who make these kinds of assumptions are "dead wrong."

✐ Be careful what you say, because if you're not, you may be putting labels on people that will get you into big trouble. For instance, referring to someone as "openly gay" might imply that you think that gay people should keep their sexual choice private. Using the expression "you people" is also a big no-no. You don't want to go up to a Jewish person, for instance, and say, "Do you people celebrate Christmas?" Not only will you be appearing ignorant, but you will create a feeling of *you* versus *us*.

❧ When you're speaking to someone who is not a native English speaker, do us all a favor, will you, and don't speak so loudly that you can be heard in the next county over. The idea is to speak slowly, not loudly.

❧ I try to explain to my staff that there are significant cultural differences when it comes to issues like communication. For instance, in America, we prize people who look you in the eye when they speak. People who don't look you in the eye are referred to as "shifty." But in many cultures, it's considered bold and inappropriate to look someone in the eye, particularly if the person you're talking to is higher up in the pecking order than you are. Similarly, here in America, we like to call people by their first names, particularly on the West Coast. We're an informal lot. But in other cultures, you wouldn't dream of calling somebody you didn't know well by his first name, particularly if that person was significantly older than you were.

❧ Try to find some common ground. Fortunately, you are working in an area where there's a built-in universality: the love of food. But maybe you could connect with the other person by playing a little soccer in the backyard on an off hour or hanging a dartboard somewhere in the workplace or showing each other pictures of your children (although, again, in certain cultures, people are much less forthcoming than Americans are about their private lives).

Mentoring

One last "team" issue we'd like to talk about here is the mentoring of those who work under you. As we said at the top of this chapter, the kitchen is a very hierarchical environment, and as you become a senior member in it, you will inevitably find people under you, often apprentices. This can be a complicated relationship, but it also can be extremely satisfying if both parties play by the rules. Your colleagues in the field take this matter very seriously:

✧ The mentoring relationship is meant to work well for both parties. For the mentor, it's a way to give back. If you love the field, this is your chance to "grow" someone, so that the field will continue to be its best. In the past, you were probably mentored. Now it's your turn.

✧ We assume that mentees learn from mentors, but there's no reason to think that it can't be the other way around. I was mentoring a kid who had the most infallible feeling for the heat of chili peppers. He was fearless and brilliant! I learned plenty from him.

✧ Mentoring people helps to keep you fresh and on your toes. The more you teach, the more you review.

✧ Neither mentors nor mentees should expect to come away from the relationship with a deep friendship. It's not a mother-daughter/father-son thing. If the friendship happens, then it happens. But the real reason for the relationship is that it's a teaching opportunity.

✐ Like anyone who's serving in a teaching capacity, a mentor has to understand that people learn best in a positive atmosphere. Give praise when due. Be measured in your criticism. Never fly off the handle or allow your criticism to be harsh. If it is, you may immediately lose the trust that is so valuable to the relationship.

We've covered quite a lot in this chapter regarding issues that have to do with getting along with other people. In the next chapter, we look at how to get along with yourself, particularly in times of high stress.

Chapter Reference

Dornenburg, Andrew, and Page, Karen (2003). *Becoming a chef*. Hoboken, NJ: John Wiley & Sons, p. 244.

Opening an Oyster

You may never be asked to open an oyster. You may never even come close to one. They are not nearly as popular today as they used to be. In New York City at the turn of the century (nineteenth to twentieth, that is), oyster stands were found all over town, and people stopped in the streets to have a dozen or two the way we might order a hot dog from a street vendor today. Those days are long gone, and raw bars are not going to factor into everyone's experience. Still, you really *should* know how to open an oyster. What if you're on a desert island? Or what if your boss asks you to open one? Doing the job the wrong way will almost certainly inflict a nasty wound on your hand. Doing it the right way goes like this:

- First, look the oyster over closely to make sure that the shell is tightly closed, indicating that the mollusk is alive, as it should be. Rinse the shell under cold running water.
- If right-handed, hold the oyster in your left hand (reverse this for left-handers). Holding the oyster in a towel will offer some protection to your hand in case of a slip. Hold the oyster knife down near the tip, and insert it between the shells at the hinged area.
- Twist the knife sharply to break the hinge.
- Next, slide the knife under the top shell, and cut through the adductor muscle that closes the shell near the top. Remove the top shell.
- Carefully cut the lower end of the muscle from the bottom shell to loosen the oyster. Make sure you remove any particles of the shell before serving.

If you've never tried to eat an oyster before, now's your chance!

Chapter 6

Inside the Pressure Cooker

s a culinary professional, you should know, at the very least, how to boil water, right? All kidding aside, boiling water is a central concern when it comes to cooking. When water is heated in a pan and the bubbles stick to the bottom, the temperature will read about 160°F. As the bubbles rise to the top, the temperature rises accordingly, to approximately 180°F. When the water starts to move slowly around the pan, it means that the temperature has reached the vicinity of 200°F. As the water jumps about furiously and tries to get out of the pan, a temperature check will reveal that the boiling point has been reached: 212°F.

We now invite you to picture yourself as water on top of the stove, if that's not too much of a stretch.

When you arrive at work, after a week's worth of long nights, your bubbles are probably draggy and may be clinging to the bottom of the pan. As the day progresses, and you've had your coffee and your stimulating interaction with your colleagues, your bubbles come alive. There you are, perking along, in the groove, with your bubbles moving around in pleasingly random patterns. Of course, as the dinner hour approaches, and "showtime" looms, the bubbles start to perk a little more restlessly. Pretty soon, Murphy's Law takes over, and everything starts to go wrong. You burn your hand on a hot pot. Your assistant drops a platter of asparagus. A customer sends back perfectly seared tuna, complaining that it's "raw." The flan that always unmolds perfectly suddenly won't budge. A tension headache is kicking in. The bubbles are wildly trying to escape the pan. You are there—at the boiling point—and it doesn't feel good, does it?

If this scenario sounds familiar, it's no surprise. After all, you've chosen a high-stress career. Some careers are infamous for their stress—air traffic controllers, bond traders, emergency room doctors—while other careers are regarded as much more low key. Working as a culinary professional *is* stressful—there are no two ways around it. The work is physically demanding, with all of the issues of operating in close quarters with other people. You are providing a service, so you have to deal with the public and the fickle appetites of your customers. You also have the ongoing pressure of having to prepare food that is pleasing to your customers, and, with food, there is little margin for error. One bad meal usually translates into one lost customer, if not more. If you're an owner-chef, you have a whole slew of other problems to confront, such as personnel issues and the vagaries of the economy. What you get in return is the joy of cooking and the pleasure and rewards that can come from being recognized for your talents. Some people have no problem with this mix of pros and cons, while others may wind up reorienting to less stressful jobs in the field, such as a food writer or a recipe tester. Only you can determine how much stress is tolerable and then reach a healthy decision about how to proceed. Whichever decision you ultimately come to, however, you will need to learn how to handle stress, both in the short term and the long term. This chapter presents many ideas and tips from fellow culinary professionals regarding stress relief and stress management.

 ## Stress: It's Everywhere

Soufflés that don't rise are stressful. Butter that burns is stressful. People who take your favorite wooden spoon without asking cause you stress. When the owner of your restaurant tells you that your cuisine is a little "far out" for customers, that causes you stress. Standing on your feet for long hours is stressful. Seeing a room with no customers is very, very stressful. Having a restaurant critic call your cuisine "uninspired" is *extremely* stressful.

All of the aforementioned is part of the life you lead, but we have to put your stress as a culinary professional in the context of your stress as a citizen of the world in the twenty-first century, which is a very stressful world indeed. Of course, people say that the world has always been stressful, and that's true. The Black Plague and the Crusades were no picnic, and running from saber-toothed tigers wasn't exactly relaxing either. But most people today experience the world as growing *increasingly* stressful, so we will take a look at this issue to see why that might be so.

For one thing, we as a society are becoming more and more sleep deprived. In the olden days, sleep deprivation was not the issue it is now, because before electrification, people followed the natural cycle of light and dark and hit the sack when darkness came. We of the twenty-first century, on the other hand, are up until all hours, working, working, working, or playing with our electronic gadgets, from DVDs to computers to treadmills and what have you.

Uniquely, the United States also has developed a kind of workaholic culture that maximizes stress. The average American worker gets only a couple of vacation weeks a year, compared to a couple of *months* of paid vacation a year for the average European worker. In the United States, too, issues of child care become a major source of stress for many American employees, with the stress factor going through the roof when children get sick and can't make it to their regular child care providers. Baby boomers are further stressed out by their unusual role as "the sandwich generation," having come comparatively late to child rearing on one end of the spectrum and often finding themselves saddled with the responsibility for aged parents on the other end. Throw into the mix the fact that many of us commute to work along highly congested thorough-fares, are grappling with the worst economy in a quarter-century, and are living in a scary post–September 11 world where terrorism is a whole new factor in our lives and you can see how stress levels are going off the charts.

Everything we've talked about thus far—all of the stress you may be experiencing in your job as a culinary professional and all of the stress you experience as a human being at this confusing moment in history—is further complicated by the high-stress events that can happen at any time of your life. A death in the family, marital problems, financial reversals, illness or injury . . . any of these by themselves can significantly add to stress, and when these events come in pairs or, heaven forbid, multiples, then the stress can become life threatening. See the chart that follows for an index of stress points:

Add Up Your Stress

Various life events can translate into increased stress. Consider the list that follows of such events, with their corresponding numerical "points," and ask yourself which ones you've experienced in the past 12 months. Keep in mind that all stress events are not necessarily negative in nature. Stress can basically be defined as a response or reaction to a "stressor," an event that signals change. Some stressors are external, such as getting fired or being in a fender bender, while others are internal, such as the agitated feelings set off by an argument. Similarly, some stress is constructive, in the sense that it gets you motivated to do something (getting married, for instance, motivates you to get to the church on time!), while other stress can have a destructive impact. To compute your stress "index," add up the points and see the "Findings" section for scoring.

__Death of a spouse, 100

__Divorce, 73

__Marital separation, 65

__Jail term, 63

__Death of a close family member, 63

__Personal injury or illness, 53

__Marriage, 50

__Getting fired, 47

__Marital reconciliation, 45

__Change in family member's health, 44

__Pregnancy, 40

__Sexual difficulties, 39

__Birth of a child, 39

__Change in financial status, 38

__Death of a close friend, 37

__Changing jobs, 36

__Foreclosure of mortgage or loan, 30

__Trouble with in-laws, 29

__Receiving an award, 28

__Starting or finishing school, 26

__Change in living conditions, 25

__Trouble with boss, 23

__Change in work hours, conditions, 20

__Change in residence, 20

__Change in sleeping habits, 16

__Change in number of family gatherings, 15

__Change in eating habits, 15

__Vacation, 13

__Christmas/holiday season, 12

__Minor violations of the law, 11

__Your Total Score

Findings:
0–149: Low susceptibility to stress-related illnesses
150–299: Medium susceptibility to stress-related illnesses
300 and over: High susceptibility to stress-related illnesses

<http://www.cliving.org/lifestresstest.htm.> For permission to reprint: <info@cliving.org>

From what we've said so far, the one thing you can be sure of is that if you're feeling stressed out, you're hardly alone. Let's hear what your colleagues have to say on the subject.

☙ I've been through hell this year—absolute hell. The restaurant I was working for went out of business— another victim of the economy. My boyfriend broke up with me—he needed his "space." My mother was suffering from asthma crises, so that I had to move back home for a month to take care of my father and my little brother. Then I slipped on a wet floor and broke my ankle. I swear, this has been the year to end all years. I finally had to get started on an anti-anxiety medication. I was trying to hold everything together, but I just couldn't. I realized that I needed some serious help, and fortunately I knew the right person to get it from.

∾ I was in a lot of trouble about six months ago, and I didn't even know it. I thought I was holding everything together—new job in a new restaurant; my daughter getting married; my parents giving up their home and moving into a life care center—but I guess I wasn't doing as good a job as I thought I was, because one day I went out to lunch with a girlfriend of mine and she said to me, "Rhonda, why are you eating so fast?" And I said, "What do you mean?" So she told me that not only was I eating so fast, but also I had barely even talked to her during lunch. Well, by the end of that day, I started to reflect on what she was saying. I realized that I had all these little telltale signs of stress, and that it was time for me to start paying attention to them. I was so glad she said something to me. It kind of snapped me to attention.

∾ I'm great in a crisis. Last year, a big water pipe burst in the kitchen at our restaurant, and I was like Mr. Civil Engineer, calling all the shots. It's the chronic, ongoing stress that I'm not so great at. It just wears me down and wears me out, and I start dragging myself around, totally without energy. I'll come home, I'll eat a bowl of cereal, and I'll fall asleep over the news. What a life, eh?

∾ When you're stressed, it's good to comfort yourself, but I take it to extremes. For instance, right after

September 11, I was cooking non-stop. I was making tapioca pudding and bundt cakes and macaroni and cheese for all my neighbors. It was all I could think of to try to make things a little better. But I couldn't stop. I got into this very compulsive thing, and when I was no longer bringing around bundt cakes to the neighbors—basically because they forbade me from entering their homes with anything else fattening—I started gorging myself on my own food. I don't want to tell you how much weight I put on, which only stressed me more.

✐ I'm pretty good at handling stress, but my girl-friend is really bad at it. You know what she does? She goes on shopping sprees. When she's having an anxiety episode, she'll run up credit card bills you wouldn't believe, buying shoes and lingerie and closet organizers and I don't know what else, and then she has a whole new bout of anxiety when the bills come in. It's a really vicious cycle.

✐ You know, we live in a world today when if you hear the word "stress," it's like, "Ohmigod, the sky is falling." I think we have to toughen up a little and realize that stress happens, and it's a normal part of life.

✐ I actually find stress to be a great aid when used properly. I have a regular gig working for a caterer, but I'm also a cabaret singer. I find the two similar in that, in both situations, there's an "opening night." I mean, I've been on jobs with my boss where we're doing an event at the Metropolitan Museum for 200 people and, to me, it feels just like when I play a club. The stress is there, sure, but it's more of a stimulant to motivate you to do what you have to do.

✍ You can't run away from stress. I had a friend who was in culinary school with me. We both went to work in top restaurants, me in Miami, my friend in Dallas. Well, she spent a couple of years there and couldn't handle the stress. She just thought it was all too fast track. So she took her savings and moved to the Outer Banks of North Carolina, where she opened up a little tearoom. You think she doesn't have stress? She's running her own business, she's dealing with personnel, and she's working just as hard as she always did. Come on, the fantasy's nice, but the reality always wins out.

✍ We all have to expect some stress in our lives. I mean, the kids crack up the car, or the tax bill is twice what you expected, or your mother-in-law's arriving for a three-month visit. That's life, and you've got to suck it up. But "some stress" is different than "constant stress." Constant stress means that you're always in a "fight-or-flight" state, and your body is paying the price. You're releasing more adrenaline than normal, you've got an increased heart flow and elevated blood pressure, more sugar from the liver, and, over time, all those little physiological changes can result in some major health problems. I'm talking about ulcers, hypertension, migraines, asthma . . . you name it.

What You *Can* Do . . . and What You *Shouldn't* Do

It's bad enough to have to cope with those life events that rate high on the stress points index, but as bad as things get, we human beings seem to have an endless capacity for making things worse. Let's see what your fellow professionals own up to on this matter.

❧ You remember all those old movies that showed men at war? The sergeant was usually somebody like John Wayne, and there were always this group of soldiers under him. One of them would be from Brooklyn, and he'd be a regular guy you could always count on. One would be the poet or the intellectual, and he'd get killed. Then you'd have the "kid," who was wet behind the ears. And then you'd have the nervous Nellie, who'd crack toward the end. Well, as a chef in a very high-stress dining room located in the Loop, sometimes I feel like John Wayne on Guadalcanal. I've got the regular guys I can count on, and the "kids" and the poet (usually an actor) who doesn't get killed but who quits when I most need him, and then I have the nervous Nellie. The one who, when the going gets tough, always starts spouting negativity. "We can't do it! It'll never work!" This is the kind of person I cannot afford to have on my team. Things get rough enough. I don't need to be swept into the black hole of somebody else's negative thinking.

❧ If you think of natural enemies—mongoose and cobra; rabbit and fox—I'd have to say that the natural enemy of stress is flexibility. It's taken me a long time—like, maybe, most of my life—to learn this lesson, but, hey, it's never too late, right? I can now admit that, for a long time—a *very* long time—I was the Queen of Mean. Everybody who cooked under me was in agreement that I was a total piece of work. I couldn't help it—I come from a long line of control freaks, and the professional kitchen is kind of the natural habitat of control freaks. I've seen people practically explode if someone comes along and salts their soup. It's just that I had these very high expectations, and if they didn't get met, I'd go ballistic. Well, don't you know I wound up with people quitting on me—on the spot, thank you very much—and before you knew it, I had bleeding ulcers. So I had to learn a new way to live—the flexible way—and even though it's always going to be learned behavior for me, I've gotten pretty good at it.

✑ Stress is very much related to what your expectations are and what your concept of reality is. I know that from my own, very painful experience. For a while, I thought I was Superwoman. I was married to a physician; I lived in a beautiful suburb; I had two young children; *and* I had a catering business. I really believed, in my heart of hearts, that I could out-Martha Martha Stewart. And I almost pulled it off, but the problem was I was living a lie. Underneath my sunny exterior, hidden inside all my wicker baskets and beneath my linen napkins, was this seething mass of jangled nerves. I couldn't hold it all together, and how did I find out? My body was telling me. I got TMJ, which is this awful neuralgic condition of the jaw that comes from grinding your teeth together when you sleep, and that's when I resolved to take care of myself.

≈ It's really important when you're under a lot of stress to make sure that you're not trying to deal with it by riding roughshod over other people. Sure, a lot has to be excused when people are under stress and things are said that you just have to let roll off your back. I mean, if you can't stand the heat, get out of the kitchen, right? But even so, we all have to watch our mouths when we're under stress. Hostile and aggressive talk is only going to make things worse, like throwing fat on the fire.

≈ If you really want to look at what you may be doing to add to the stress in your life, consider your relationship to the word "No." It's the most important word in the English language, and you've got to get good at saying it. "No, I can't. My daughter is getting married this weekend." "No, I'm sorry. I have a dental appointment scheduled for that time." "No. This is not a task I feel that I should be asked to do, as I've already explained to you." Without that word, "No," your defenses are barely there.

≈ One of the things that has always caused me stress is the sense of frustration that I experience when I tell somebody something that I think is constructive, and they just don't do anything about it. We had a guy on our team who would let things fall on the floor and wouldn't pick them up until he was all done with whatever he was doing. I said to him,

"Arnie, that's dangerous. Somebody could slip and fall on it," and he's like, "Oh, yeah, right." But does he pick it up? It would make me crazy. But then I came to realize that you really can't change people. They are who they are, and it's not your job to change them. In fact, trying to, and not succeeding, only causes you stress. You can change your own behavior—nobody else's. So when I realized that Arnie wasn't going to change, I went to my boss and complained. I put the brakes on something that was causing me stress, and being proactive that way did me a lot of good.

৵ If you want to try to get a grip on your stress, start separating it out. Don't think of your life as one big mass of stress. In fact, take the stress points test and see how you do. I was feeling stressed out recently, and I took the test and I discovered that I just wasn't making enough money. My bills were piling up; my debt was getting bigger; and I was getting scared. In fact, the stress around my financial difficulties was causing me to panic, but when I took the stress points test, I found out that I didn't have marital difficulties, I didn't have health problems, I had no problems with the law, I wasn't moving . . . I was just hard up for money, and my total stress points index was down in the low-medium range. So after that I felt like, okay, you can get through this. Other people have it a lot worse, and they survive. You can do it. And I did. Sure enough, almost immediately, things started getting better in the financial department, and the stress started to go away.

❧ If you're feeling a lot of stress, and you're getting headaches or you're running to the bathroom every five minutes or you feel like you can't get a deep breath or know what it's like to relax anymore, then you need to ask yourself what you're doing to help yourself. Are you treating stress as a medical problem? Are you exercising, doing deep breathing, meditating, or whatever else will bring you relief? If those things don't work, have you investigated the possibility of using medication to ease your anxiety? Talk to your physician immediately about your problem. The longer anxiety goes untreated, the more damage it can do.

 *Stress Relief*

As good as you may become at avoiding stress, let us reinforce reality here: you cannot escape it. There is no fairyland village where stress does not occur. Trappist monks in remote mountaintop monasteries feel stress, because it is, after all, part of the human condition. So let's roll up our sleeves and start talking about practical, everyday ways of dealing with it.

Deep Breathing, Anyone?

You're running around the kitchen like the proverbial chicken without a head. Orders are mounting. One of your coworkers is mouthing off. The mushroom stock has disappeared. Your partner is calling you on your cell because your dog just bit a deliveryman. Your heart is pounding, your head is pounding, and you feel like you're going to explode! What's the first line of attack? Let's listen to our culinary professionals:

❧ Always start with deep breathing. It's the thing I go back to the most—free, easy, healthy, no strings attached. Start by inhaling deeply through your nose, filling up your lungs. Then hold that breath while you count to six. Don't just let it out all at once, but exhale slowly, counting once more to six. Then repeat, and continue to do this for several minutes. You'll see how much better you feel so soon.

❧ It's not like you need a lot of "tricks" when it comes to deep breathing, but one little Zen-type thing that I do to enhance the activity is I say this little chant while I'm breathing. I'll say to myself, "In with the good" on the inhalations and "Out with the bad" on the exhalations. It's just a good, simple way to rid my mind of toxins.

❧ In culinary school, I was really stressed out half the time. I mean, believe me—it was a stretch for me to be going to culinary school in the first place, and when I had to do some of the stuff I had to do, like the math part of food science, for instance, I was just freaking out. Anyway, I made this good friend on the second day of school, and he had done a lot of meditation and stuff, so he taught me about breathing. But in the beginning, when I'd do it on my own, I'd start hyperventilating—that's how wound-up I was. I'd get all light-headed and even more stressed. It wasn't long before I was able to get my breathing under control, but the hyperventilating is a good thing to know about just in case it happens to you.

The Healing Power of Communication

We talked in the last chapter about the importance of communication in interpersonal relationships. Communication also serves as a very important way to break down and control the stress that may be ruling—and ruining—your life. Your colleagues in the field see it as a life skill you can't be without:

✍ Sometimes it just takes a word or two from somebody nearby to get you back on the right path. I was going through some really dark days a couple of years ago. I had a high-pressure job as an executive chef, and my marriage was coming apart at the seams. Looking back, I realize that I was a walking time bomb, completely bottled up, jaw set, the veins in my neck popping. Finally, Georges, my *sous chef* at the time, asked me if I was okay. "What do you mean?" I demanded. When he told me how tense I seemed, it just sort of snapped me out of myself. I swear, if we hadn't had that communication—if Georges hadn't cared enough to talk to me—I don't know what would have happened.

✍ Working the long hours I do in this very intense world of food, I really feel like I need the input of "civilians." I spend as much time as I can with my friends and family, because I can open up with them. And being able to open up and share your feelings about things that trouble you goes so far toward breaking down the stress.

❧ I've moved four times in three years for my work. From what I hear, that's not so atypical in the food world. So when I wind up in a strange city, it can be pretty isolating. Sometimes the only people I know are the people I work with, and I don't always want to be with the people I work with, thank you very much. So what I've learned to do is to go to the Internet. I find a chat room—not *that* kind of chat room, but one where people talk about world events or *Buffy the Vampire Slayer*, which I happen to adore, or whatever else interests me at the moment, and I make my cyber-friends. And they really are friends. Even though I'm not face-to-face with them over a cup of coffee, I can still talk very personally to some of them, and I think the anonymity of it can actually be kind of a help sometimes.

❧ My stress at work was getting so bad that I felt if I didn't talk to somebody in a real way pretty soon I was going to take my Sabatier™ to the next person who came too close. So I found a church with this great pastor who I felt so comfortable talking to. It doesn't matter what religion you are, but the point is that the spiritual community can be a very good place to find the kind of renewal and communication that helps to beat the stress in your life.

❧ If you're suffering from stress overload, you may need counseling. I did. I got the name of a wonderful woman, a psychiatric social worker that a friend of mine had been to see, and she's helped me enormously. Don't try to always do it on your own. If you had a bad tooth, you'd go to a dentist, right? Well, if you've got too much stress in your life and you're feeling exhausted or angry or hopeless, it may be time to seek out the services of a mental health professional.

꩜ Communication is vital. Saying what you're feeling takes you beyond just feeling it and into the realm of doing something about it. But who says that communication has to be with a human? My dog, Sadie, who's an English Springer Spaniel, is the perfect friend for me. She listens to me whenever I speak, she doesn't speak back, and she gives me unconditional love. If you're a cat person or a bird person, that's fine too.

Get Out of Your Head

Although stress can be stored in any part of your body—your neck, your back, your jaw—the real place it's stored is in your head. A good strategy for dealing with stress is to get *out* of your head and *into* the pleasures that you can find in physical activities. Here is how some of our culinary professionals keep themselves in shape:

꩜ Nothing keeps stress under control the way regular, vigorous exercise does. I speak from experience, because I've had a long history with anti-anxiety drugs, and, believe me, I'm not knocking them. But I still do better when I let'er rip on the treadmill. I've got Gladys Knight and the Pips on full blast, and I'm running full blast, and I'm sweating full blast, and my stress is out the window right then and there. And not only right then and there—there's real carryover. Those endorphins linger on and make you feel more potent and much more in control of your life.

🌿 Exercise is great for reducing stress, but some people manage to turn exercise itself into a stressful activity. You don't have to be Carl Lewis out there, you know. The idea when you exercise is to enjoy yourself. For you, that might mean getting off the treadmill and getting onto the tennis court or the dance floor or putting on some in-line skates. Just make sure it's fun and that you do it regularly . . . and you probably won't do it regularly if it isn't fun.

🌿 I try to do something physical every day, even if it's just getting out for a fast stroll for 15 minutes. I see some of my staff go out for a smoke break, and I say to them, "Why don't you go for a walk instead? Do your heart some good?"

Laughter and Other Therapies

When you're feeling stressed, be creative! Your colleagues have some interesting ideas:

🌿 Laughter is the #1 weapon against stress. It just flushes your system clear of it. Nobody can feel stress when they're belly laughing.

🌿 I have an arsenal of comedy tapes that I know can bring me down from a stressful day in record time. These include *Tootsie, Some Like It Hot, The Honeymooners,* my favorite *Seinfeld* episodes, the Marx Brothers, *This is Spinal Tap,* and, of course, the Three Stooges. When

Moe pokes Curly in the eye, I don't care how bad my day has been—I'm a goner.

❧ A friend of mine gave me a present of Loretta La Roche tapes for the car. She's this advocate of laughter as therapy, and she's very funny and very real. You can check out her Web site at <http://www.stressed.com>.

❧ I find that keeping a journal helps me maintain a perspective on my stress. It's a reflective activity, and when you reflect on something, what happened at 10 in the morning doesn't seem quite so bad when you think about it at 10 at night.

❧ My greatest stress reliever is working in my garden. For some people, it's their coin collection or building wooden birdhouses or knitting or whatever, but the point is that hobbies are very beneficial. They're that special time you give yourself where you're totally absorbed in something that is causing you pleasure, not pain.

❧ Beauty helps. I live in a little cottage by the shore, because I need beauty on a daily basis. It drives the stress right out of my life. For some people, buying fresh flowers is enough beauty to do the trick, or even a Zen sand garden on the desk might work. It's up to you.

❧ Is it too obvious to mention? I'm talking about vacations. Sometimes people forget to take them. Often, if you work for yourself, you don't even think about taking a vacation. But just a few days away breaks the pattern and goes so far toward freeing you from stress. Any kind of break in your daily pattern can feel like a vacation. Take a few days off, stay home, go for a walk in the park or take the ferry boat across the river or go to the beach, and you'll see how much better you feel.

As we've said, the thrust of this book is holistic health. Stress is part of the problem, but there are other serious pitfalls for those working as culinary professionals. In the next chapter, we examine those pitfalls and explore the many ways that you can be good to yourself and your body.

A Perfect Batch of Rice

Almost as shrouded in myths and contradictions as the hard-boiled egg, the cooking of rice can lend itself to all kinds of pitfalls. Improper cooking, which usually is the result of an incorrect ratio of rice to water, can result in sticky, wet, dry, or burnt rice. Rice can be cooked successfully on the range, in a steamer, or in the oven. It can be cooked in large quantities of water, like pasta, but it will lose most of its nutrients that way. The Chinese method of placing a dish towel between the pot and the lid to absorb moisture is a good trick. In all of our journeys through the food world, however, we have come across one method that always turns out perfect and unusually delicious rice. Here's how to produce eight servings of this "perfect" rice:

3 tablespoons butter
1/2 cup finely chopped onion

2 cups raw rice
Salt to taste
Cayenne pepper or Tabasco™ sauce
3 cups chicken broth
Parsley
1 bay leaf
1 sprig fresh thyme or 1/2 teaspoon dried

- Preheat oven to 400°. Heat two tablespoons of butter in a saucepan. When it melts, add the chopped onion and cook it, stirring, until it wilts.
- Add the raw rice, and stir until the grains are coated.
- Add salt to taste, a pinch of cayenne, or a dash of Tabasco™.
- Add the chicken broth with a *bouquet garni* of parsley sprigs, the bay leaf, and the thyme. Let the broth come to a boil. Cover the saucepan, and place it in the oven for exactly 17 minutes.
- Remove from the oven, and discard the *bouquet garni*.
- Add one tablespoon of butter to the rice, and blend it in.

This rice is so nice that it is almost a revelation. And it's totally foolproof.

Chapter 7

An Ounce of Prevention

e've been talking about stress—how it impacts on you and how you can relieve it. But stress is only part of "the big body picture." In this chapter, we delve deeper into the many ways that you can fall into bad habits and how you can bring yourself back to wellness.

As a culinary professional, you will find yourself in situations specific to your field that can seriously tax your wellness. For starters, you are involved in very physical work. You are constantly on your feet, lifting heavy pots, bending down, reaching, and using repetitive motions as you whisk and whip. In addition, you are working under the stress of performance pressure. You also work long hours and may be suffering from sleep deprivation. Plus you're surrounded by food and drink and may overindulge in both of those departments.

When you're dealing with issues of health, the best policy is to be preventative rather than reactive. In other words, it's a lot harder to deal with a problem *after* the fact than *before* the fact. We identify areas of risk and then offer strategies for how to avoid those risks. Keep in mind too that we are working from a holistic orientation. Again, by "holistic," we are invoking the idea of "wholeness," which emphasizes the organic or functional relation between the parts and the whole of something. If we take a holistic approach to our lives, we are emphasizing ourselves as whole persons, not as a set of isolated functions. In looking at ourselves holistically, we take into account the mind, the body, and the spirit. We explore how these forces interact and impact on each other. To neglect one will, over time, negatively affect the others. We don't want that to happen.

We begin our discussion with food. What better place to engage the interest of the culinary professional?

You Are What You Eat

The relationship of the culinary professional to food is remarkably complicated, because there is little in the life of the culinary professional that is more important than food. Food is your first love, the focus of your creative inspiration, your "meal ticket," your claim to fame. On the other hand, you have the same relationship to food that everybody else in the world has:

you need to eat to stay alive. Your daily minimal requirements for protein, calcium, iron, and what have you are no different than anyone else's. So how do you strike a balance between food as this exalted goddess you worship and food as the fuel that keeps you chugging along? Some of your colleagues relate their experiences on the subject next.

The Language of Food

Just listening to culinary professionals talk about their relationship to food and food preparation can be illuminating. For example:

❧ I've been a total "foodie" ever since I could hold a spoon in my hand. There's nothing I loved more in life than to sit at my grandmother's kitchen table and to have her bring me fresh, hot *palacsinta*—that's Hungarian crepes, if you haven't come across them—which she'd fill with cottage cheese and her homemade apricot *lekvar*. I'm sure those little bits of heaven are what made me want to become a chef. But sometimes I worry that food has *too* much prominence in my life. It's not only my expanding waistline that concerns me, but it's what's happening in my arteries.

❧ The relationship of people to food is one of the most complicated relationships you can imagine. It's laden with joy, guilt, memory, sensuality, revulsion . . . you name it. Keeping that complexity in mind is an important part of a chef's work, and sorting out your own personal relationship to food is an important part of each individual's life work.

☞ When you come down to it, cooking is about sharing and intimacy. My customers eat what I have wrought with my own two hands. It is a gift that I give them, and their pleasure in my work is the gift that they give back.

☞ Food is fun, and food is work. It's creative and it's formulaic. It's extraordinarily elaborate and utterly simple. Anyone involved in the world of food recognizes that some of the greatest meals you'll ever eat will be a sparklingly fresh piece of fish cooked on an open fire, or a sublimely ripe mango eaten out of hand. The endless opportunities we have available to us with regard to food as a species on this planet make eating a never-ending adventure and sometimes an occasion for wretched excess.

☞ Cooking makes me feel like I'm a totally organic part of the world. When I hold a fruit or a vegetable in my hand, I feel connected to God.

☞ Cooking is about community. The best feeling in the world is to be cooking with a group of people, making a meal for everyone to share.

☞ Cooking is a great haven for me, because it requires absolute concentration. When I'm home and I'm cooking and the phone rings, I let the machine pick up. The caller can wait; my omelet can't.

The Perils of Food

As glorious as food can be, however, there's also a dark side to it. Again, let's hear from your colleagues.

❧ I have a confession to make: I was much more drawn to food before I became a professional. I loved the honesty and the simplicity of good home cooking, like my mother used to make. She'd put a perfectly roasted chicken on the table, with wonderful vegetables and this killer almond cake she'd make for dessert, and I thought, what could be better? She really was my inspiration for going into the field. But now that I've been working—in a number of different situations, mind you—I don't find that honesty as much as I'd like to. Some of the restaurants that I've worked in have taken some pretty shabby shortcuts and have served food that is well below the quality I'd feel comfortable eating myself. When it comes to food, the first rule is to be careful what you eat. You can get pretty sick putting the wrong things in your mouth.

❧ In my training as a chef, I've spent quite a bit of time abroad in France and Italy and Spain. I've noticed that people in those cultures rarely eat to excess. They seem to have such a sensible relationship to food. I mean, it's all-important to them, but they don't abuse it. Here at home, on the other hand, so many people have a very sick, addictive relationship to food. That's all they think about, even as soon as they finish a meal.

❧ I've worked in kitchens where the portions that go out to the customers are absolutely gross. Even though all of the restaurants I've worked in have supposedly served *haute cuisine,* the owners have demanded that we "supersize" the portions, as if we're competing with McDonald's or Denny's. So we've got something like garlic mashed potatoes on the menu—who doesn't these days, right?—but the helping is like the size of a small cabbage. And the really depressing thing is that the vast majority of our customers lick their plates clean, no matter how much we pile on.

☞ I tell you what drives me crazy: how many different food "needs" are floating around these days. I mean, it's one thing to be diabetic and not be able to handle sugar or to suffer from hypertension and to have to avoid salt. But when I have customers coming into my restaurant, which is a very fine establishment, if I do say so myself, and start asking for fat-free salad dressing and egg-white omelets, I feel like, "Special orders do upset us!"

☞ One of the sicker things going [on] in our society is the way we criminalize food. I get these ladies in who shudder at the idea of a sweet at the end of the meal, and if there should be anything fried on the menu, heaven forbid, they look at us like we're pushing heroin. Can't they see that any food taken in moderation is perfectly acceptable?

☞ You've heard of fear of flying and fear of heights and fear of germs and fear of black cats. But do you know what constitutes one of the most prevalent fears in our society? Fear of fat. First of all, to be fat in a culture that's dominated by the stick models that fashion so reveres is a terrible disgrace. Fortunately, we're starting to see gorgeous large women like Queen Latifah taking care of that hang-up. But so many people today think that it's a terrible thing to ingest any kind of fat at all. I try to explain to them that fat is healthy for you. It's quick energy, and it satisfies the hunger for much longer periods of time than carbohydrates do. There are so many people out there who abjure fats but stuff themselves on low-fat or non-fat yogurts, cheeses, gummy bears, and what have you. Who do they think they're kidding?

✍ There are good fats and bad fats. When you go to culinary school, you discover the joys of goose confit and the perfect crust you get on fried chicken from using lard and stuff like that, but hey—let's get real. Those things aren't really good for you on a daily basis. You know that, right? The good fats, like those we get from olive oil and nuts and stuff, are really, really good for you. One of my favorite good fats is avocado. Sliced avocado on whole-grain or sourdough bread with lime juice and cilantro is as good a sandwich as you'll find, and it's perfectly good for you.

✍ Where did this idea of three square meals a day ever come from? The point is to eat when you're hungry. In Europe, nobody has a big breakfast. The idea of people eating eggs and bacon and sausage and pancakes and Danish in the morning would be abhorrent to most Europeans. Coffee and perhaps a dry rusk is their speed. Similarly, a great many Europeans go home for a big lunch (dinner) and for supper will have just a little salad or some dried meats or cheeses and bread.

Watching Your Weight

There comes that time in the life of many a chef when the hard truth has to be looked straight in the eye: you've eaten too much over too long a period of time, and you're overweight. Your pants won't close, and your scale reading can't be possible! It's an occupational hazard, for you're around delicious food *all of the time!* Your fellow culinary professionals share some of their strategies next.

✒ In our field, when you're constantly exposed to irresistible foods, it's hard not to be carried away. I have my own private mantra: *Do not eat when you're not hungry.* Most of the time you're doing that, you're just trying to make up for stress, which can be better dealt with anyway by a few minutes of deep breathing or a walk in the fresh air. You'd be amazed how much easier it is to keep your weight under control when you pay attention to your stomach hunger instead of your mouth hunger.

✒ Eating slowly is a good way to start losing weight. And if you're serious about food—which obviously most of us are—you're certainly more inclined to eat slowly and to really taste and savor what you're eating. I find that if I eat slowly and chew my food thoroughly, I eat a lot less, and my stomach is a lot happier.

No matter what your eating issues may be—whether you're putting on weight or whether you're having digestive problems or whatever—it will all be significantly remedied if you remember to drink a lot of water. Water is so vital.

Water, Water, Everywhere . . .

As you probably know, 60 to 70 percent of the human body is comprised of water. Nothing is more important. At least that's the way our culinary professionals feel:

When you're running around a steaming hot kitchen, you simply have to remember to stay hydrated. Think about how much water we lose in that kitchen as we sweat and strain. Those fluids have to be replaced if we're going to keep functioning.

I've always heard that you're supposed to drink at least eight glasses of water a day, so that's what I aim for. I don't go anywhere without my water. I always keep it with me, in a thermos, and I make a point of drinking *before* I get thirsty. Drinking after you're thirsty is a catch-up game, and depending on how much you've allowed yourself to dehydrate, catching up can be hard to do.

If you're looking to make smart choices, stay with water when you're thirsty. Other liquids, like

---

tea and coffee, can act as diuretics, actually caus-ing water to *leave* your body. Also, why do you need the calories in colas or the chemicals in diet colas or the expense of drinking fancy juices or bottled shakes when water is so cheap, so healthy, so nonfattening, and so refreshing? And, lovely as it may be, wine is definitely *not* the thing for hydrating yourself.

꒰ I agree with what the others have to say about the importance of water, but, like everything else, you don't want to overdo. I've heard of people who were drinking, like, gallons of water a day, and that can be dangerous too.

Dieting

In our culture, dieting has become an obsession . . . a very dangerous obsession. For those in the field, it's a real sore spot:

꒰ I despise the word "diet." It's one of the most overused words in the English—no, make that the *American*—language. Everybody is on a diet *all the time*. Now when I feel like I need to take off a few pounds, I don't start weighing whatever I eat on a scale or consuming disgusting amounts of cabbage or watermelon or drinking some hideous glop or doing whatever the hot trend of the moment is. I simply cut back—in half—the amount I usually eat, and generally I lose the undesired weight.

✎ The diet industry is just such a scam. You're supposed to spend all this money buying all these products that don't work, and you can make yourself really, seriously sick in the bargain. No thanks! And I hate the child-like position that dieting puts you into. That coy thing—was I "good" today? Was I "bad"?—it's so demeaning.

✎ Not only are most weight reduction diets completely worthless, but so are a lot of these eating and exercise regimens that people subscribe to. If you're going to go with a program, at least ask a few important questions first. Like what percentage of people who enroll in your course complete it? What percent lose weight? What percent keep it off at a year, three years, and five years? And what kind of medical problems do you see from people who have taken your course?

✎ Before you even start with dieting, I think you have to look at the issue of body image. We, as a society, tend to have a warped image of what the human body should look like. We're surrounded by ads that tell us that men should have "six-packs" and women should be a size two. Well, take a walk down any city street, and you'll see how few size twos or fours [are] out there. In fact, American men and women are getting more overweight, not less. Our eating habits and our sense of our body image both need to be addressed.

❧ I've always been large. My mother, my sisters, my aunts, my cousins, and my grandmother on my mother's side are all large too. We're living testimony to the inescapability of genetics. I knew I was never going to be one of those 90-pound fashion models. I'm not made that way. One of my legs is bigger than most fashion models are. Is that something I should be punished for? Besides, I love food. So I decided to be a chef. A big fat woman chef. Wanna make something of it?

❧ I believe there's such a thing as a set point when it comes to weight. It's what you were meant to be. I'm 5'3" and my set point is 158 pounds. I've gone down to 128 and popped right back up like a cork. So now I feel like, "Okay—that's who I am." That's the package I come in. My friend Amy is 5'5" and weighs 98 pounds. That's who she is, and she's luckier than I am because our society values the way she looks. But, to me, it's like we're two different breeds. A greyhound looks one way—long and thin—and a Labrador retriever looks another way, with thick legs and a barrel chest. Well, do you know anyone who doesn't love a Lab? More to the point, do you know anyone who's always saying to a Lab, "Look at you! Don't you have any self-control? What's the matter with you? If you had the willpower, you could change." I doubt it.

❧ I went to a workshop on body image, and they had us do this fascinating thing. They asked each of us to write down the three people in history we most admired and would like to sit down and have a conversation with. Well, everybody wrote down people like Martin Luther King, Golda Meir, Louis Armstrong, Albert Einstein, Mark Twain, Eleanor Roosevelt. Nobody wrote down Twiggy or Kate Moss or Courtney Cox or anybody like that just because they were skinny. In fact, the skinniest person on the list was Gandhi. But he wasn't on any list because he was skinny!

Getting Fit . . . Staying Fit

As a culinary professional, you're one step ahead in the fitness game because you're *moving* all day long. You're constantly using up calories straining that soup, unmolding that summer pudding, pounding those chicken breasts, and what have you. Compared to someone sitting at a computer terminal for eight hours, you're Spider Person! But let's get real—even with all of the running around that you do, it's not enough to balance out the amount of calories you take in, is it? There's only one real solution to this mathematical problem: exercise.

When it comes to exercise, whether you love it or hate it, there's no ignoring it. Just look around and you'll see people running, jogging, walking, hiking, swimming, weight lifting, and in-line skating . . . exercise is clearly a national trend. But let's not get too carried away and act as though everyone in the lower 48 states is some kind of Olympic hopeful. The truth is that although the physically fit are ever-more visible, we, as a nation, are becoming ever more sedentary. Makes sense, since year to year, as a nation, we are becoming increasingly overweight.

Exercise is vital to the way we live our lives, not just for purposes of weight control, but because it allows us to think more clearly, to combat stress, to ward off depression, and to secure that precious personal time that too many of us sacrifice without the discipline of something like a fitness program. Factoring exercise into an already busy life may not be easy, but it is necessary. We've asked your fellow culinary professionals to share their thoughts about exercise. They say the following:

✐ The first piece of advice I would offer anyone is not to raise the bar too high . . . maybe not even over your head, to start out with. You're just trying to get something good going for yourself. Something good generally means something in the neighborhood of three to five exercise sessions a week, anywhere from a half-hour to an hour per session. That sounds doable, doesn't it?

✐ Are you the kind of person who thinks that exercise is boring? If so, join most of the rest of the human race. Most exercise, particularly of the aerobic variety, *is* kind of boring, at least until the endorphins kick in. I counter the boredom by picking a repetitive motion that I don't hate too much. I do the treadmill while I watch CNN. That keeps me informed and fit in one fell swoop. A lot of people like aerobic dancing because it burns off a ton of calories and it's fun. You've got to shop around.

❧ I always look for ways that I can up my exercise output. Like I'll take two steps at a time when I'm walking up stairs . . . or, better yet, I'll walk the whole way instead of taking an elevator. When I go to the mall, instead of circling for 20 minutes looking for a parking spot that's close to the stores, I'll park really far away and walk 20 minutes. It's that kind of thinking.

❧ For me, it's made a big difference to have an exercise buddy. Exercise Anonymous, you know? Somebody to help keep me in line, to share the agonies and ecstasies with.

❧ One thing that's become clear to me is that if I really want exercise to be a part of my life, I'm better off doing it the same time of day every time, or otherwise I'm probably going to be interrupted.

❧ There's an expression I've heard—*train, don't strain*. If you're hurting, or if you're breathing too hard to be able to carry on a conversation, you may be doing something wrong. To make sure you're doing what you should be doing, check with your physician before starting any kind of exercise program.

❧ I like to track my progress. I keep a chart of what I've done from day to day, week to week, month to month. When I'm feeling burnt out on exercise, this record of how far I've come inspires me to go further.

❧ I found it almost impossible to integrate my work with my fitness routine. So hard in fact that I gave up my job as a *sous chef* in a downtown restaurant and took a job instead as an executive chef with a Fortune

500 company. This way, I get to use the corporate health club. What a perk!

. . . And Then There's Sleep

When it comes to wellness, nothing is more important than sleep. Sleep is that behavioral state characterized by little physical activity and virtually no awareness of the physical world. It is a blessed refuge that some of us, unfortunately, have difficulty accessing. Scientists don't know why humans need to sleep; all they know is that they do.

Research has shown that after as few as six days of reduced sleep (four hours or less a night), the body is limited in its ability to metabolize carbohydrates. In other research experiments, it has been shown that laboratory rats deprived of sleep will die in two to four weeks. Some scientists and physicians theorize that the purpose of sleep is to reduce certain chemicals that have built up in the body during the waking hours. In any case, the human need for sleep is programmed into us, and the vast majority of human beings either sleep in one long snooze of six to eight hours or one bout of five to six hours, with an hour-long nap in the afternoon. The timing of sleep is profoundly connected to the cycles of light and dark. Humans are a diurnal species; thus they sleep at night. Some people need 10 hours of sleep a night; others do just fine on five or six. Think about your own sleep habits. So many of you in this field work late into the night, disrupting that natural cycle of light and dark and how it relates to sleep. Do you find yourself having problems with getting to sleep? Do you often wake up? Do you drag yourself around during the day? If so, you're not alone.

Sleep "Do's"

Follow these do's and don'ts of sleep from your colleagues, and dreamland should be just a few eye flutters away.

🌊 I was having a lot of sleep issues because of my late hours, and I actually went to a sleep clinic. The #1 piece of advice they gave me was to stick as best as I could to a regular schedule. Even if you just get six hours a night instead of the recommended eight, it's better if you take those six hours in their regular time slot.

🌊 It may sound like common sense—and it *is* common sense—but the fact is that you should try to relax before you get into bed. Now some people interpret that to mean that you lie there, in your bedroom, watching TV till you doze off, but that's not the idea. TV might be good at distracting you, but studies have shown that the electronic stimulation is not very good at relaxing you. Instead, have a warm bath and get into bed to read a book . . . a boring one, preferably. Listen to some tranquil music—that Celtic New Age stuff is perfect. Whatever you do, give yourself a chance to really unwind, and then let the sleep come.

~ I'm a nut when it comes to room temperature. I get restless if the room is too cold, and I don't even come close if it's too hot.

~ I'm very sensitive to noise. I have a "white noise" machine that plays sounds of nature, like waterfalls and ocean surf, and I also use earplugs when necessary. There are some excellent pliable earplugs on the market now.

~ If you do run into trouble sleeping, it's better that you don't get up to watch TV or turn the lights on to read. Try to stay with your normal light-dark schedule, and just remain in the dark, listening to music if you want.

~ Naps are great. Even 15 minutes dozing on the couch in front of the TV can go a long way. But I've been told that if you're going to get into napping, it's better to try to nap at the same time every day. Otherwise you can interrupt your sleep schedule and wind up more tired than ever.

Sleep "Don'ts"

Avoid these sleep pitfalls, otherwise you could wind up walking around in circles all night. Your colleagues say the following:

~ Here's a real no-brainer: steer clear of caffeine. At the very least, don't have it after four in the afternoon, and don't have it at all if you've been experiencing sleep problems. A lot of people I know in the food world scoff at this and think that decaffeinated coffee is some kind of bad American joke. But not sleeping is no joke either. There are wonderful decaffeinated coffees and, better yet, some marvelous herbal teas. I'm hooked on a passion fruit tea right now, and I don't miss the caffeine at all.

Sleep Deprivation

Sleep deprivation is a serious medical condition that affects over 47 million Americans. Although it can have any number of bad effects on people, two of its most significant dangers follow:

❧ *Driver fatigue.* According to the National Highway Traffic Safety Administration, over 100,000 automobile accidents occur each year because of sleep-deprived drivers. Research has shown that driving while sleepy is as dangerous as driving while intoxicated. According to researchers in Australia and New Zealand, drivers who went without sleep for 17 to 19 hours operated their vehicles worse than drivers with blood alcohol levels of more than 0.05 percent—the legal limit in most Western European nations.

❧ *Impaired glucose tolerance.* A study conducted by the University of Chicago Medical Center in 1999 indicated that sleep deprivation could dramatically affect the body's ability to metabolize glucose, leading to symptoms that mimic early-stage diabetes. This impaired glucose tolerance can eventually lead to actual diabetes, obesity, and hypertension.

✐ Most chefs I know claim to have cast-iron stomachs. Nothing bothers them, they crow in the most macho way imaginable. But I see them popping the antacids behind the pantry door. Few of us are immune to the distress involved with highly spiced foods, and when you're working at getting your sleeping habits back into a good place, that's not the time to indulge in vindaloo curries, Scotch bonnets, or Szechuan hot pots. Highly spiced foods can do an excellent job at keeping you up all night.

✐ Be careful about when you exercise. I find late afternoon is best, but I'm good in early morning too. Just don't do it close to bedtime, because if you do, you can kiss that night's sleep good-bye.

✐ Hey, I've used sleeping pills, and no doubt about it, they work. But you should never be on them unless you're under the care of a doctor, and in any case, you shouldn't be on them for more than four weeks at a time.

 *Bad Habits*

Now that we've looked at some of the ways people can make themselves feel good and healthy and strong and full of energy, let's look at how they can do the opposite. Chief among people's self-destructive behaviors is substance abuse, both alcohol and drugs (which often go together, by the way), and smoking.

The wide availability of alcoholic beverages can be a significant problem for those working in the field. Drinking in moderation can easily lead to drinking in excess, particularly when alcohol is used to relieve stress. Here are some thoughts from your colleagues on how to curb bad habits:

❧ Amazing wines surround me at all times. That's quite a temptation. At first I thought I was just being an oenophile—a great connoisseur of the grape—but as time went on, I realized I was drinking for reasons that went way beyond connoisseurship. I was drinking because I needed to drink, because I couldn't handle the pressure. And when I got pulled over for DWI, my reality was staring me in the face.

❧ I never drank at work. But I drank when I got home. Two, sometimes three, glasses of wine. No biggie, I told myself, but it started getting hard for me to get up in the morning. And, more than that, I realized that I was drinking because when I got home at night I was often feeling depressed or anxious about all the pressures I had at work, and the wine was taking the edge off for me. It's when you use wine for that purpose—to take the edge off, rather than to enhance the experience of a rack of lamb, or whatever—that you have to start examining where you're coming from.

❧ I make a rule for myself: never drink alone. To me, that smacks of problems.

❧ Working in the field, it soon becomes apparent to you how many people in our culture have a drinking problem. Being aware of it made me aware that I had a problem too, and I did something about it. I went to Alcoholics Anonymous, and I got it under control. I don't drink anymore. And this decision impacted on the kind of cooking I do. I used to be a very traditional, French-inspired cook. Now I'm macrobiotic!

♒ What is there to say about smoking? It's a "feelthy" habit, non? It really is. Fortunately, most restaurants forbid it now. It's so inconsistent with the real enjoyment of food anyway. No one should ever start smoking in the first place. It's so much easier never to start than to give it up.

♒ I really wish more people understood that switching to low-tar, low-nicotine brands is not going to make a bit of difference. The low-tar brands just make you puff harder and longer and more often to feed your nicotine habit.

♒ What about the expense of smoking? Unbelievable!

♒ You've got to realize that stopping smoking is not going to be any picnic. Nicotine is a really powerful, addictive substance, and kicking the habit is hard work, nothing less. You may need to use nicotine gum, patches, or whatever. Just tell yourself it's one day at a time, or one hour at a time, or one minute at a time—whatever you have to tell yourself to get through the hard parts.

♒ If you want to stop smoking, get some good advice about how to go about it. Your doctor or your dentist is a good place to start. You could also log on to the Web sites of some of the big organizations for directions. Try the American Lung Association <http://www.lungusa.org>, the American Heart Association <http://www.americanheart.org>, or the American Cancer Society <http://www.cancer.org>.

Physical Presentation

We wrap up our discussion of wellness with a few choice words on physical presentation. As we mentioned several times before, you are involved in a field where you are doing a lot of lifting, bending, reaching, and standing. All of that takes its toll on you. Some words of wisdom from your peers follow about how you can face the physical challenge most effectively:

🖋 I grew up as an army brat, and my dad, even though I love him dearly, is a little bit of a Great Santini, if you know what I mean. He's very much the career military man and has a strong idea of how things should be done. Well, one thing he really drummed into me and my brothers and sisters is the idea of good posture. We had to stand a certain way—head up and chin level with the floor; neck elongated and balanced directly above the shoulders; chest out and up; shoulders level, spine straight; abdomen flat; hips level horizontally. He'd drill us on this stuff, and we'd hate it, but you know what? It's saved my life working in this field. There's so much wear and tear on your body, and good posture is, like, the first line of defense against bodily woes.

✍ The way you stand is important, but just as important is the way you sit. We don't all get that much sit-down time, but when we do—when we're trimming string beans, let's say, or prepping potatoes—and we're sitting down, we should always remember to sit with our rears to the rear of the chair. Remember that: rear to the rear. Sitting all sprawled out is not good for the body.

✍ I know station chefs who use a cushioned mat under their feet at their station. They say it really saves them a lot of fatigue.

✍ Shoes! Shoes, shoes, shoes. There is nothing like a good pair of shoes with a lot of arch support to preserve your strength and energy. Some of our young people come in with sneakers, and forget it—they're wiped. I tell them to get one of those new outdoorsy boots that all the manufacturers are putting out now. They come with tons of arch support and are super comfortable. For some of us, orthopedic shoes are a real lifesaver too.

✍ If you're on your feet all day long—and do I have to tell you that, in this field, you *are* on your feet all day long?—then you have to administer to your feet when you [get] home at the end of the day. Maybe you'll want to soak them in some Epsom salts. Give them a massage after showering, and then thoroughly dry them, especially between the toes. Put on a little antiseptic foot lotion or natural foot powder afterwards— that's very beneficial. Regular visits to the podiatrist help a lot too.

❧ Fit your work to your body, not your body to your work. That means if you're doing a lot of repetitive motions—bending, stretching, lifting—experiment with what feels good and what doesn't. Watch others on the staff, and have them watch you to input on the way you're using your body. Sometimes it's hard to see for yourself what weird ways we move in!

❧ Bend at the hips or the knees, not at the waist, particularly if you're lifting something heavy.

❧ Picture a flamingo. How does it stand? On one leg. When you've been standing for a long time—as you are wont to do in this field of work—you can get a little relief by placing one foot on a chair or stool for a while. You'll see the difference.

❧ If you're really feeling exhausted, try to find someplace where you can lie down on your back, just for five minutes, with your head resting on a rolled-up towel and your feet up on a chair. It's a lifesaver.

❧ There are certain ergonomic issues that you can deal with on your own, and then there may be others that you have to deal with across the board. Your kitchen needs to be assessed if there have been injuries or if people are feeling uncomfortable working in the environment. Things may need to be rearranged to minimize reaching, or there may need to be more room between stations. The management will have to work together with the staff to find solutions to these problems.

So far in this book we have addressed the universal concerns of working culinary professionals. We now turn to the specialized fields for more tips from the trenches.

Chapter References
University of Chicago Medical Center study: www. uchospitals. edu/news/1999/19991021-Sleepdbt.php
NHTSA study: www.fmcsa.dot.gov/safetyprogs/ research/focussums.htm

---

Caramelized Onions

If we had to name one "secret" ingredient to get diners to love you, it would be these amazing caramelized onions that you can use in omelets, in frittatas, in pasta tossed with sheep's milk yogurt, on mashed or baked potatoes, with rice, risotto, and polenta, in sandwiches, focaccias, and pizza . . . just about everywhere but ice cream. (Hey—why *not* ice cream?) Make up a big batch, because they keep well in the refrigerator—up to a week. They're an inexpensive, easy-to-make item that feels like a luxury and makes people happy. Follow these directions, and you'll be happy too:

1 tablespoon unsalted butter
1 tablespoon vegetable oil
1/2 teaspoon salt
1 teaspoon brown sugar
2 pounds of onions, peeled and sliced 1/4-inch thick
1 tablespoon water
freshly ground black pepper

- Heat the butter and oil in a 12-inch nonstick skillet over high heat.
- When the foam subsides, stir in the salt and sugar. Add the onions, and stir to coat, and then stir occasionally until the onions begin to soften and release some of their juice. This will take about five minutes.
- Reduce the heat to medium, and cook, stirring frequently, until the onions are nice and browned and slightly sticky. This will take roughly 40 minutes more.
- Remove the skillet from the heat, stir in the water, and season to taste with the pepper.

Chapter 8

Cooks and Chefs: The Basics, Part 1: Hygiene, Sanitation, and Safety

If you've been waiting hungrily for certain kinds of information, then you might regard this chapter and the one that follows as the main course. Or should we say the "crash course"—"All About Cooking 101." We present the basics—what every cook should know. Of course, we wouldn't presume to try to tell you everything you need to know about cooking in a few dozen pages. That's what you've got those big fat textbooks for. But we do feel that we can give you a very fast, very digestible overview that can serve as a good point of reference.

In the next chapter, we discuss basic techniques all cooks should know. Before we start, however, we feel that it is absolutely critical to hear from your colleagues about hygiene, sanitation, and safety. As we said at the very outset of this book, when you cook for people, you are literally taking their lives into your hands. Outbreaks of salmonella or E. coli or incidents of leaving foreign objects in food, such as pits, shells, or, heaven forbid, broken glass, have hurt or even killed people. Of course, the percentages of people who eat in restaurants compared to those who die from eating in restaurants are, thankfully, not even close. But ask yourself how you would feel if a tragedy came about as a result of your neglect. Did you know there was once an outbreak of food poisoning in Sweden that affected over *8,000 people!* Tragically, 90 of them died. This is a serious business, ladies and gentlemen. So let's begin.

Safety

Safety first. It's a good motto—you've heard it before. Nowhere is it more applicable than in the kitchen. When you think about it, the average kitchen is a pretty hazardous place—knives and machines and heavy things to drop on fragile toes, people running around in a small space. Did we mention fire? Boiling water? Hot oil?

Microbes? Is this quickly turning into a horror movie? *Friday the 13th Meets TGIF®*?

Of course, it needn't be. A well-run kitchen is as safe a place to work as any, and we are learning more and more all the time about how to ensure safety in the kitchen environment. Let's start, however, by focusing, as promised, on "the basics."

Hygiene and Sanitation

We'd rather go to a scrupulously clean diner any day than a four-star restaurant where shortcuts and deceptions are the rule for hygiene and sanitation issues. Food-borne illnesses such as hepatitis and salmonella are extremely unpleasant at best and quite deadly at worst. The following section will provide a good overview to the sort of hygiene and sanitation concerns to keep in mind.

Personal Hygiene

There is no better place to start than with your own personal habits. Let's hear what your colleagues have to say.

ᕤ We can't control everything in the kitchen. For instance, we can't control someone accidentally knocking a pot off the stove. It happens, no matter how well-developed our systems are. But one thing we can control is our own personal hygiene, and by doing so, we can hugely cut down on the risks we pose to ourselves and to others.

✐ Let's start with a sparkling clean wardrobe, okay? Each day you go to work, your uniform should look like it's almost as good as new. There is no excuse for gravy stains. Dirty uniforms carry germs, you know.

✐ You're going to need to invest in a wardrobe that will allow you to change off whenever something gets dirty. For most of us, that means multiples of four—four chef's caps, four white jackets—and multiples of six, with six neckerchiefs, aprons, and "rubbers" (linen kitchen cloths). You can probably get away with three pairs of pants or three skirts—whatever makes sense for you.

Laundry List of Stain Removers

If you're lucky, someone takes care of your laundry and makes it white again. If not, here's what you need to do:

✐ **Wine.** Stretch material over a bowl, and pour boiling water through.

✐ **Berries.** Sponge with lemon juice, flush with water, and allow to dry.

✐ **Blood.** Soak as soon as possible in salted water. Wash in cold water.

✐ **Butter.** Gentle scrape away residue, then dampen the stain and rub powdered detergent on it, scrubbing between your thumbs. A dry-cleaning fluid may be necessary.

🌀 **Chocolate.** Remove excess chocolate with a scraper, then sponge with cold water or soak for 30 minutes in an enzyme prewash solution. Rub detergent into the stain, and then flush with cold water. A final treatment with a dry-cleaning fluid may be necessary. (Ah, but chocolate's worth it, isn't it?)

🌀 **Coffee and tea.** Blot, then rinse with cool water, followed by detergent rubbed in and then the usual machine washing.

🌀 **Egg.** Scrape off solid matter, and then soak in a non-metal container with an enzyme solution for up to eight hours. Drying will set the stain, so make sure it's out first.

🌀 **Oil.** Olive, canola, safflower . . . you name it. Scrub with distilled water and soap.

🌀 **Meat juices.** Sponge with cold water, and wash in cold water.

🌀 Keep your nails trimmed. Overly long nails are great shelters for all kinds of bacteria.

🌀 Let's not forget the time-honored chef's hat. For women *or* men (a ponytail on a man is no assurance that his long hair is not going to wander). Is there anything less appealing than somebody else's hair in your food?

✐ Okay. This may seem entirely unnecessary, as there are big important-looking signs in every bathroom in every restaurant in the country. But employees must wash hands! Seriously, folks . . . we're not kidding.

Wash Those Hands

At a pivotal point in history, physicians discovered a direct link between the conscientious washing of hands by medical personnel and the reduced mortality rates among their patients. The same precautions apply to culinary professionals, who must become thoroughly "immersed" in the proper techniques for hand washing.

When to Do It:

- Before starting work
- After using the lavatory
- After handling raw food
- After touching one's hair, coughing, sneezing, blowing one's nose, and touching any sort of waste or refuse
- Often during the day, as it occurs to you. You cannot *overwash* your hands!

How to Do It:

There's a proper procedure. Follow these steps:

- Rinse your hands.
- Wash hands thoroughly with approved soap.
- Rub the soap through your fingers, your thumbs, and all over your palms.
- Rinse thoroughly.
- Use paper towel or hot air dryer to dry your hands.
- Turn off the tap with a paper towel.

Safe Food Handling

We've said it, but we'll say it again: poor sanitation and improper food handling can result in sickness and mortality. It also can result in the mortality of your establishment. Nothing will end a restaurant's life quite as quickly as a serious outbreak of food poisoning. Can you blame the consumer? It's not exactly easy to work up an appetite for a three-course meal in a restaurant that has recently sent people to the hospital. For our culinary professionals, safe food handling is something that must always be kept in mind:

✔ If you start to think about what you can be infected with when you go to eat in a dirty restaurant, it boggles the mind. In addition to salmonella, an infected food handler can wind up spreading hepatitis, typhoid, diphtheria, and you name it. Does it happen often? No, thank goodness. But the point is that it *can* happen.

✔ Safe food handling starts with careful food examination. Look at what comes into the kitchen, and carefully assess whether it's suitable for human consumption. Start with smell—that's what your nose is for. It absolutely astounds me when we use a purveyor who delivers bad chicken—which means, of course, we never use that purveyor again. Always smell the ingredients you're using. (And obviously I don't mean burying your nose in the food you're about to prepare.) A chef's best friend is his or her nose.

✒ I keep an eye out for any discolorations on poultry. Not a good sign . . .

✒ When vegetables and fruits are delivered, they often have garden soil adhering to them, particularly if they're very fresh. This soil, which can carry bacteria *even if it's organic*, cannot come into contact with other foods in the kitchen. The fruits and vegetables have to be prepared in their designated areas.

✒ Cans that are rusty, corroded, or that bulge suspiciously should never be used.

✒ Food storage is a very important issue. Some foods do not keep well. Dishes like aspics, for instance, that you might have on a buffet table, are made with agar-agar, the very raw material that's used in the lab to grow cultures! Unless you're planning to do an interesting science experiment, dispose of any aspic that never got chosen off the buffet table and chalk it up to waste. Better that than getting sick. Better *anything* than getting sick. I mean, have you ever had food poisoning?

✒ Look around your kitchen, and assess the environment. Are the counters constructed of impermeable materials, like marble or stainless steel? They should be. You certainly don't want counters of absorbent materials like wood that can harbor bacteria. And what's your waste disposal system like? Is someone cleaning the garbage cans . . . inside and out?

✎ Cleaning up as you go along and the correct washing of dishes are important issues. The drill for washing dishes goes like this: pre-clean with a little scrubbing and scraping; clean thoroughly with detergent; rinse; destroy bacteria with a sanitizing procedure; rinse again; and let the dishes air-dry.

✎ Always wash the tops of cans before you open them.

✎ Here's one to have tattooed on your forehead: every time you taste food while you're preparing it, use a clean spoon. This way you won't be spreading bacteria from your mouth to the dish.

✎ Use separate towels for your hands and for the dishes.

The "V" Word

That's "V" for "vermin" . . . and nothing will close down a kitchen faster than if a health inspector sees indications of these wretched creatures. As someone who works in a kitchen, you should be fully aware of the telltale signs of the presence of vermin. These include the following:

✎ *Droppings*. Ugh . . . but true. Mouse droppings are small, dry, and seedlike. Rat droppings are naturally larger and moist when fresh.

🖋 *Damage*. Any sign of gnawing anywhere—on foods, but also on wood, soap, or even pipes—is one of the surefire signs that there's a mouse (or worse) in the house.

🖋 *Smears*. Ugh, again. These are the marks left by the greasy, dirty fur of the rodents as they touch surfaces.

🖋 *Disappearance of bait*. Well, it won't take a genius to figure out that it wasn't a trout that got that piece of cheese from the mousetrap.

Immediate measures to take once the presence of rodents has been discerned include: (1) removing any sheltering structures lying around, such as cartons, crates, or rubbish offering good hiding places; (2) filling rat holes with steel wool, concrete mixed with glass, or other such impenetrable materials; and (3) storing all food in rodent-proof containers. Of course, an exterminator should be contacted immediately for further measures.

🖋 Cockroaches are it for me. I can never think about a place the same way after I've seen roaches there. I mean, they've got this awful smell, and they're just so gross. But did you know that even though it's possible for roaches to carry bacteria like shigella or salmonella, they're not nearly as bad in that respect as the common housefly is?

✒ If you ever watched a close-up film of what a fly does in the kitchen, you'd lose your lunch right then and there. We make war on flies in our kitchen, and for the most part, we come out ahead.

✒ Here's a good tip on disinfectants: a hot disinfectant beats a cold disinfectant by a country mile. In other words, hot Lysol™ is going to work a lot better for you than cold Lysol™.

✒ Good hygiene and sanitation in the kitchen is a continuing education issue. Everybody has to work toward the same goal, and the best way to do that is by having real training sessions, visual aids like posters, awards and prizes for meeting goals, and so on.

Cleaning Tips

There are a million good cleaning tips. Everyone has his or her favorites. A few of ours follow:

✒ Disinfecting sponges is important. Some do it in the dishwasher, but that's not the best way to kill bacteria. Some try the microwave, but you can burn a sponge or impurities can spark a flame. A three-minute soak in boiling water is the best method.

✒ Clean a can opener by running a sheet of paper towel through it.

✒ Here's an easy way to clean a pan: fill it with salted water, and set it over high heat until the water boils. As the temperature of the water increases, the gunk will loosen, and you can scrape it free with a wooden spoon.

✍ Use cold water to clean bowls that have had dough in them.

✍ Clean up spilled oil by sprinkling a layer of flour over the oil and waiting a few minutes for absorption to occur. Using a paper towel or a brush if glass is present, move the flour around until it absorbs all of the oil, and sweep it into a dustpan with a broom. Finish up by spraying the area with a glass cleaner.

✍ To clean a blender, fill it three-quarters full with water to which dishwashing liquid has been added. Turn on the blender for 30 seconds, then rinse well.

✍ Ketchup is great for cleaning copper. Applied directly and allowed to stand for five minutes, it will take off tarnish easily.

Food Handling

Becoming aware of what can go wrong with foods is a very important part of a cook's development. Tips from your fellow culinary professionals regarding food handling follow:

✍ Although there's a movement toward room-temperature food in certain kinds of Mediterranean *cucina fresca* preparations, most of the time you'll want to have your extra quantities kept warm on a range, in the oven, or in some other kind of warmer, or cold, in the fridge. There are major risks to letting food hang around at room temperature.

✐ Stay on top of any new guidelines with regard to the proper internal temperatures for meat, fish, poultry, and so forth. You've got to make sure that you kill those little microbes you know.

✐ When a serving dish is empty on a buffet table, clean it out before adding more food, or better yet, use a fresh, clean dish.

Thawing Techniques

Don't thaw food at room temperature. It isn't safe. The outside can accumulate all sorts of harmful bacteria before the inside is thawed. Use the following techniques instead:

✐ Thaw your frozen foods in the fridge. Allot time for it. It's the safest way.

✐ If you have to thaw something quickly, run the frozen item, in its original wrapper, under cold, running water.

✐ Microwaves can be useful for thawing purposes, as long as you follow the manufacturer's instructions closely.

Safety in the Kitchen

As we said at the top of this chapter, the kitchen can be a minefield, as you run the gauntlet of knives, potential burns, collisions, and whatnot. Your colleagues provide a wealth of tips on how to avoid accidents.

✐ First and foremost, your establishment has to have a sound, thought-out, and written-out safety policy that expresses itself in easy-to-understand language, multilingual if necessary, and that's available for anyone and everyone to see. It needs to include the names of those individuals who are responsible for fire safety and prevention, for personal injuries, for OSHA [Occupational Safety and Health Administration] compliance, for first aid, and for safety training.

✐ In my experience, I've found that a kitchen that has a generally high morale also has a good safety record. Kitchens where there is a lot of infighting, or where people are obviously not very interested in each other's welfare, are dangerous places, not only emotionally and psychologically but, ultimately, physically as well.

✐ What causes accidents? Think about it. The big rush is probably the number one culprit. When too many people are running around trying to get too much done in too little time, accidents *will* happen—no two ways around it.

✐ The first thing I do when I get a fresh young face in my kitchen is go over the basic use and handling of tools. I wouldn't send a kid out with a chain saw to cut down trees without doing a thorough training session, and I wouldn't put a kid to work as a station chef without making sure that he or she had some basic knife-handling expertise.

✤ Look, you've got some dangerous equipment in the kitchen. You've got meat-slicing machines, bread-slicing machines. Accidents will happen, and they'll basically happen to people who haven't been trained sufficiently and don't know what they're doing, which is inexcusable, or to people who have been doing it so long that they stop paying sufficient attention, which is highly avoidable.

✤ If you have to, you can cut costs here and there on your ingredients. You can pull back on the cheese, you can use cheaper cuts of meat—good cooks know how to compensate for these money-saving measures. Where you can't cut back on is on anything having to do with safety. You can't get by with inadequate lighting or poor ventilation or an overheated environment that leads to dulled reflexes. If you try to cut back on that, you will really start to pay the price.

✤ Somebody needs to take on the job of looking at the structure of your kitchen, on a periodic but not infrequent basis, and making sure that it is safe. For instance, broken or loose floor tiles will cause workers to trip. And a worker tripping with a pot of bouillabaisse will probably not only injure himself but a coworker as well.

✤ I've worked in some kitchens where the staff comes in wearing ribbons in their hair or jewelry dangling from their wrists. Come on! The kitchen is no place for such things. Ribbons can catch fire; bracelets can get caught in machines. Tragedies can occur around such inappropriate work attire. So get with the program, folks.

🎕 *Mise en place, mise en place*. Everything in its place, boys and girls. If you use something, put it back where it belongs when you're finished. Not only does an organized kitchen allow you to produce better food, but clutter control goes a long way toward the reduction of accidents.

🎕 You want a surefire recipe for how to have an accident? Leave drawers open. There's an accident waiting to happen.

🎕 Don't take shortcuts. Don't say to yourself, "Well, I've got this knife in my hand anyway—why bother with a church key when I can just pry the lid off that jar with this? Then wham! The next thing you know, there's a major cut on your hand, and you're on your way to the emergency room.

🎕 Store heavy items on low shelves. If you're taking a heavy pot down from a high shelf, it could slip out of your hands, fall on your head, and cause major head trauma.

🎕 Don't even think about slicing frozen food. When the food thaws, *then* you can slice it.

🎕 Falls are bad, bad things. Tie your shoes, don't wear long skirts that you can trip over, wipe up spills *immediately*, and use real step stools to get things down from high places, not some improvised chair-and-telephone-book-thing construction.

Falls and Collisions

You're running around and so are your coworkers. That's a prescription for an accident. Keep the following pointers in mind to preserve your safety:

✐ Walk, don't run.

✐ Stack trays and trolleys so you can see over them and know where you're going.

✐ Use the right doors. "IN" means you're entering. "OUT" means you're exiting. Pay attention!

✐ If there are overhangs or potentially excellent places to hit your head, outline them with bright tape or some other eye-catching device.

✐ I've personally never encountered a professional kitchen where knives were just kept loose in the drawers, but I've heard they exist. Obviously knives should be in a drawer by themselves or, infinitely preferable, in a knife rack.

Cutting-Edge Information on Knife Safety

Probably more injuries are caused in the kitchen by improper knife techniques than anything else. Keep the following points in mind at all times when using knives:

～ A sharp knife is safer than a dull knife. Dull knives require you to use more pressure; they create more frustration, and they are more likely to slip.

～ Keep fingers away from the sharp edge of the knife blade.

～ Never hold an item in your hand when cutting it. You may see people cutting a potato this way, or an apple, for instance. Bad, bad idea.

～ Never cut with the knife blade facing your body.

～ Make sure your hands are dry before using a knife. This will prevent slippage.

～ Carry knives point down.

～ Don't try to catch a falling knife. You're not a circus performer.

～ Never use a knife for a job that it is not intended for, such as opening a jar.

～ There are major safety issues regarding the cleansers and chemicals we use. Prolonged exposure to chemicals may cause allergic or immunological reactions. You might be able to use natural substances in place of some of those potentially damaging chemicals. For instance, maybe you could use lemon peels or cinnamon sticks steeped in water instead of those noxious air "fresheners." Maybe you can use baking soda to clean a surface instead of some caustic scouring powder. White vinegar works wonders on most things too.

❧ Never mix cleaning chemicals. You can set off a chemical reaction and produce something really dangerous, like chlorine gas, for instance.

❧ Fire poses an ongoing safety concern in the kitchen. Grease fires are particularly scary. You should never fill a deep fat fryer to more than a third of its capacity, and they need to have lids in case things veer out of control.

❧ This is so obvious it's almost insulting, but make sure you have fire extinguishers that work.

Avoiding Burns

Follow these steps to protect yourself against burns and scalds:

❧ Make sure you've got a good pair of oven mitts handy at all times. One of the best oven mitts you'll ever find is a pair of welding gloves that you can get at the hardware store or an auto supply shop. They are made of thick, heat-resistant leather, and they come with long gauntlet cuffs that protect against burned wrists. Because they are designed to allow you to work with your hands while wearing them, they offer lots of control and flexibility. And they're cheap.

✐ Keep the handles of your pots and pans turned toward the back of the stove. This prevents your knocking into them and sending them flying off of the stove—a recipe for disaster.

✐ When you take the lid off of a pot, always lift up the far edge of the lid first. You could get scalded if you do it the other way around.

✐ When adding food to hot oil, make sure that the ingredients are dry. Blot any moist ingredients, for the water will make the oil spatter, and you could be burned.

✐ Stand well to the side when you're opening an oven door, because 500° hitting you square in the face can really hurt.

✐ If you want to check an item that's in the oven, pull out the rack first. Don't reach in to get the item. The interior of ovens is very hot, remember?

✐ One of the scary things that can happen in a kitchen is a gas leak. As soon as you smell gas, turn off the stove, open the windows, and have everyone go outside. Then call the gas company . . . from outside.

✐ If you're ever relighting a pilot light, here's something very important to remember: light the match first, then turn on the gas to light it. If you do it the

Kitchen Fires

Fires are apt to break out in the kitchen—it comes with the territory. You need to know what to do in case that happens.

✎ *On a range.* Immediately turn off the heat. Cover the pan, or douse with salt or baking soda. (Baking *soda*, not baking *powder*, which could make the fire worse.) Under no circumstances should you try to douse the fire with water or a Class A fire extinguisher, which will make the grease spatter and could badly burn you.

✎ *In an oven, a broiler, or a microwave.* Turn off the appliance, or disconnect it from its power source. Keep the door closed until the fire goes out.

If you cannot put the fire out easily, call the fire department immediately. Also, under no circumstances should you try to carry a pot or pan with burning contents to the sink. You could burn yourself or drop the pan, causing an even bigger fire.

other way around, the gas is accumulating, and that's a really bad idea.

This chapter is a start regarding safety and sanitation in the kitchen. All through your career, keep these vital issues at the forefront of your consciousness. Now let us turn to our next chapter, "Cooks and Chefs: The Basics, Part 2—The Art and Science of Cooking."

Another all-purpose tool that every cook should have in his or her shed is a basic vinaigrette. This marvel of chemistry, in which acid and oil come together so well, can be used not only on salads, but on cold meats, vegetables, fish, broiled or grilled food, and more.

Like any preparations of great simplicity, the secret is in the ingredients. You must start with an extra-virgin olive oil. Experiment with different olive oils until you find one that is truly special to you. You can vary your vinaigrette as the mood strikes by using part walnut oil or hazelnut oil or a seasoned olive oil. From the oil, proceed to a top-quality vinegar. Different vinegars go with different salads. Champagne vinegar or white-wine vinegar go with pretty much every-thing, but at times you'll want the taste of balsamic, sherry, or rice vinegar. You also can substitute lemon juice for the vinegar, but you will need more of it, as it is less acidic.

Many cookbooks will tell you that the standard ratio for making vinaigrette is three parts oil to one part vine-gar. Don't take this as gospel. Certain vinegars are milder than others, and certain olive oils are stronger. You may even find that your best vinaigrette comes in at two parts oil to one part vinegar. You'll have to experiment.

Other flavors? It's endless. Any fresh herb, ginger, garlic, tamari, honey, cayenne, a touch of curry, may prove interesting. For the basic vinaigrette, however, we recommend shallot and Dijon mustard. The formula follows:

1/2 cup extra-virgin olive oil
3 tablespoons vinegar (you may need more)
Sea salt and freshly ground black pepper
1 teaspoon Dijon mustard
1 large shallot, peeled and cut into chunks (see note below)

- Combine all ingredients except the shallot in a blender, and blend approximately 30 seconds, until you achieve a creamy emulsion. At this point, taste the preparation and see if it needs more vinegar. Add it carefully—no more than a teaspoon at a time—until you get the acid-oil balance you're looking for.
- Add the shallot, and turn the blender on and off a few times until the shallot is minced. Taste and adjust the seasoning.
- Yield: 3/4 cup

Note: There is some confusion, in the food world at large, about what constitutes "one shallot." Some people will tell you that it refers to the whole head. Others will say that it refers to the clove. We are referring to the clove in this recipe.

Chapter 9

Cooks and Chefs: The Basics, Part 2: The Art and Science of Cooking

*C*ontinuing with our crash course in the basics, you'd better buckle your seatbelts for this chapter, because we're going to take you on a whirlwind tour, with lots of helpful little hints along the way. Again, keep in mind that we can only do so much here. There are many "basic" issues that even though they may be basic are too complex for us to deal with in the context of this chapter. The mathematical principles involved in cooking are one good example. It is crucial to know how to convert a recipe for four into a recipe for 40, but you will have to get that information elsewhere. Here we provide a quick "taste" of a lot of different basic issues. Think of it as a *dim sum* luncheon—you get a small bite of many different things.

Nutrition

As a professional cook, what should your starting point be? Some would say flavor, while others would say value. Good answers, both, but you won't find a better answer than nutrition. An awareness of nutrition really becomes an issue of ethics for the culinary professional. The real point of eating, after all, is to provide yourself with the nutrients necessary to sustain life. Enjoying your food, having a wonderful interlude with friends or family, and discovering the cultural byways of other lands are all good reasons to cook and to eat. But as we say, the bottom line when it comes to eating is getting what you need nutritionally. Let's hear how our culinary professionals handle nutrition:

✐ As a cook, I don't feel that I have to read the *Harvard Medical School Newsletter* to learn that added zinc in the diet is important to replenish hair follicles, or whatever. Not that there would be anything wrong with reading the *Harvard Medical School Newsletter* and staying on top of the latest in nutrition. But for those who don't want to go quite that far, a good starting point in a discussion of nutrition is the proverbial "balanced diet." All cooks should understand what that is and plan menus accordingly.

꙳ You've seen the Food Pyramid bit so many times, but don't worry—you don't need a calculator to figure out a balanced diet. The key to a balanced diet is to serve good fresh foods in season, to let your diners choose from a nice wide variety of dishes, and to cook so that as many nutrients as possible are retained.

꙳ Obviously the importance of nutrition depends a lot on the kind of culinary position you hold. If you're a chef in a retirement community, for instance, the issue of nutrition is paramount. If you're a caterer whose work is mostly weddings, nutrition isn't the biggest issue on your mind, because you're not feeding customers on a regular basis. If they don't get riboflavin at a wedding, it's not going to kill them, right?

꙳ Nutrient loss in cooking is an important issue, and all chefs should be aware of it. Protein generally is not lost in cooking. Even if you cook a steak until it's absolutely gray, it's still going to retain its protein content. The danger is that the patron may reject that steak, and so the protein from that steak is never going to enter the patron's body.

꙳ Vitamins B and C are the most likely to be lost in cooking because they are water-soluble vitamins, as compared to Vitamins A, D, E, and K, which are fat soluble. So you need to know what you're doing around Vitamins B and particularly C.

꙳ To ensure that you retain as much Vitamin C as possible from your vegetables, don't prepare them way in advance. When you shred a cabbage days in advance of serving it, it will lose a lot of its vitamin content. Soaking vegetables will lead to the same kind of vitamin loss.

✎ Cook vegetables and fruits in the least amount of water possible. I know this is in direct opposition to the French method, which has you throwing green beans into a big vat of boiling water, and that's delicious, but it results in a great deal of vitamin loss, and that's just not right in my book.

✎ Steaming is a great way to cook vegetables. It probably protects the vitamins more than any other method, and it's very much in favor these days. You really should consider offering steamed veggies on your menu.

✎ Rapid cooking preserves vitamins. A rapid boil cooks vegetables more nutritiously than a simmer.

✎ Salt leaches out vitamins. Salt *after* cooking.

✎ If you're really concerned about nutrition, consider using less fat in your cooking. Fat is pleasing to the tongue, and when you've tasted vegetables cooked in goose fat, for instance, per the French method, your pleasure meter may go through the roof. But very few people today are willing to sacrifice their health—and their arteries—for such taste sensations. Experiment with lower-fat cooking methods like poaching and steaming. There are also some amazing non-stick pans on the market today, which even make sautéing a less artery-clogging option.

✐ Don't be overly reliant on salt. A lot of chefs are criticized for undersalting, but I personally would rather err in that direction. Using really fresh, high-quality, and flavorful ingredients is one way to become less reliant on salt. For instance, a gorgeous, delicious tomato is a taste revelation without salt. Also, spices like ginger and chili peppers and all those fantastic flavored vinegars on the market will help wean you from the salt shaker.

✐ Study and educate yourself with regard to nutritional information. Learn how to read the nutritional information on packages, for starters. It's not enough that your food tastes good. It has to *be* good for you too.

Developing a Taste

Being sensitive to tastes and flavors was cited often as the most important part of a chef's development. You'll be interested to see what your colleagues had to say about this:

✐ To my way of thinking, the very first and most important thing a chef has to do is to develop a real sense of taste and an awareness of flavor. You have to know about heat and sweetness and saltiness and bitterness. You have to really understand the impact of a jalapeno or paprika or cumin. It's a very complex process, and it takes time . . . but it's what cooking is all about.

have to always, always, always be thinking
...ste. Not just when you're experiencing the
hig... ...ike the Beluga caviar or the *foie gras*, but when
you're eating a grilled cheese sandwich. Is that a bit of
mustard in there? Is that a bit of tarragon mustard?
What about that fingerling potato? How does that
differ—*in taste*—from a Red Bliss or a Yukon Gold?

✏ Any taste is made up of a variety of tastes. Tasting
wines [is] the perfect example. Is there apricot in there?
Citrus? Licorice? Tobacco undertones? Taste is so
complex.

✏ Most people—even those who've been to culinary
school—will tell you, when asked, that there are four
tastes: sweet, salty, bitter, and sour. What about "pun-
gent"? What about "hot"? What about "aromatic"?

✏ You want to become so sensitive to taste that
when you write a recipe, you can taste it in your head.

✏ Taste everything—every day! Never assume that
things are the way they are supposed to be. I can guar-
antee you that most of the time they're not. The only
way you know is by tasting.

Menu Planning

Menu planning is one of the most creative and important aspects of the culinary arts. The number one rule
of menu planning is to keep in mind the needs of your
diners. If you're working in a school lunchroom, you're

not going to be offering calves' liver and sushi. If you're working in a retirement home, you're not going to plan a menu around corn dogs and tacos. If you've got a lunch counter business going, forget soufflés. You have to tailor your menu to your customer. Here's how others in the field approach menu planning:

🎝 I think it's important to be known, first of all, for using really fresh, wholesome food. A lot of cooks get overly ambitious and start layering menus with all kinds of exotica, and, in a word, they bite off more than they can chew. I started out working in a little restaurant in Concord, New Hampshire. It was started by a local woman, and we only had 12 tables. The menu was very limited—three entrees a night—but everything was wonderfully fresh and simple and beautifully prepared. It was like going to the home of a fine cook and knowing that nothing was going to be served that the cook herself wouldn't sit down to eat. My boss developed a loyal clientele that followed her as she grew, and now she has one of the best-established restaurants in the state.

🎝 I hate a menu that always stays the same. It just bores me to tears as a cook, so you can imagine how the customers feel about it. I mean, we have to hold on to certain signature dishes, or people will raise a stink if they're not there. Heaven forbid we shouldn't have our famous lime chicken or our coconut rice pudding. But we're always adding and experimenting.

🎝 If you have salad on the menu, as you should, plan on serving it to your customers before the entrée.

Even though it's more traditional and I think more elegant and sophisticated to have the salad after the main course—and I will always serve it this way when I'm hosting in my own home—98 percent of your customers will expect their salads before the main course. That's just the way it is.

✐ If we're talking about basics, one of the most basic principles of menu planning is balance, particularly in terms of flavor. For instance, you don't want garlic in the appetizer, garlic in the soup, garlic in the main dish, and garlic ice cream for dessert. You want to vary the flavors in a refreshing and interesting way. Same holds true for textures. I once went to a dinner party where the host served a cream soup, fettuccine Alfredo, and Bavarian cream for dessert. I went home dreaming of a nice crisp Granny Smith apple.

✐ Appearance is a big part of the eating experience. Visual excitement goes a long way in making a meal memorable. That's why we garnish dishes with edible flowers or radicchio leaves, or why we form a dessert into a beautiful architectural statement. Similarly, a pork chop, while it may taste delicious, is not particularly memorable to look at, so we want to liven up that plate with brilliant green broccoli and a pickled crab apple.

✐ A very important aspect of menu planning is economy. How can you utilize all of the food you've purchased? Unused food will "eat up" your profits, so you have to take into account the complete utilization of food when you're planning a menu. If you are serving beef, for instance, what are you going to do with the trimmings? Will you use them in a terrine or pâté? Will you use the bones to make stock? What about those leftover egg yolks or egg whites? What are you going to do with those?

🖋 Another aspect of menu planning that relates to economy is the use of leftovers. Of course, in a restaurant, we don't want to use that word . . . at least, not to the customer. But let's face it—we're not going to throw perfectly good food away. So in planning your menu, if you've served roast chicken one night and have a bunch left over, then you may want to offer chicken potpies the next night or a Chinese chicken salad.

🖋 If you're using a costly and perishable item in a dish, like shitake mushrooms, let's say, you might want to either rethink the recipe and eliminate the perishable item or create some other dishes that also utilize the pricey item so you can maximize your investment. Keep in mind, however, that you don't want the menu to show shitake soup, shitake crepes, and shitake omelets.

🖋 Truth in advertising applies to menus big time. You're going to get into mucho trouble if you label something as "fresh" if it's frozen, or as "imported" if it comes from Sheboygan. "Homemade," "jumbo," "prime"—these are all labels that have specific meanings. Don't use them loosely.

Basic Cooking Methods

As promised, we're just going to dip into the basic cooking methods. Hopefully, you're well beyond this information. If not, it's never too late! Cooking methods come in two basic forms: moist heat and dry heat.

Moist-Heat Cooking

Moist-heat cooking methods include poaching, simmering, and boiling; steaming; and braising.

Poaching, Steaming, and Boiling. These very healthful methods involve cooking in water or some other seasoned liquid, such as broth or wine. The culinary professionals we spoke with had these tips:

✎ Although you've surely heard of boiled beef, you generally don't boil foods if you don't want the proteins to break down or you don't want the form of the food to be broken down by the rapid bubbling movements. Boiling is great for vegetables and starches like rice or pastas. For other foods that use moist-heat cooking, you'll want the lower temperatures of simmering. Boiled beef is actually simmered beef.

✎ Poaching is wonderful for fish. Poached salmon with a dill sauce is one of the most elegant buffet dishes imaginable. Of course, poached eggs are pretty terrific too, even though a lot of cooks are scared off by them.

Poached Eggs

You can't have Eggs Benedict without poached eggs, so make sure they're in your repertoire. Use the freshest eggs for the best results. Fresh eggs maintain their shape better. If you find yourself without eggs that are notably fresh, add one teaspoon of salt and two teaspoons of distilled vinegar to one quart of water.

1. Bring water to a simmer, not a boil. Boiling the eggs will toughen the whites.
2. Break your eggs one at a time into a dish, and slide them into the simmering water against the edge of the pan.
3. Simmer three to five minutes.
4. Remove the eggs from the pan with a slotted spoon.
5. Drain. With a kitchen scissors, trim off ragged edges for a neat presentation.

✑ I find that the best approach when simmering is to bring the liquid to a full boil first. When you add the ingredients, the temperature usually goes down anyway, and then you can just maintain the simmer.

✑ Keep in mind that "steaming" does not only refer to cooking over boiling water. You're also steaming something when you're essentially cooking it in its

Perfect Baked Potatoes

Where did the idea of baking a potato wrapped in foil come from? Not only does it make for an inferior outcome, but you also have the added expense of the foil. Here's how to do it right. Start by choosing *starchy* potatoes, not waxy ones. Russets are a good choice. Scrub the potatoes well, and pierce the ends to let steam escape. If you like your skins crisp, leave them dry. If you prefer them somewhat more tender, rub with oil . . . but go lightly. Place the potatoes on sheet pans or on racks in a preheated 400° oven, and bake until done, about one hour. You'll know they're done when you squeeze them lightly and there's some yield. Make sure to wear oven mitts when squeezing. After all, did you ever hear the expression "hot potato"?

own moisture. Cooking fish fillets *en papillote*—in parchment or foil—is a good example of what I'm talking about. Baking a potato in foil is another example . . . although you won't get nearly as good a result as if you bake the potato *without* foil.

✣ Braising is another moist-heat method that's really wonderful and that's somewhat neglected, if you ask me. I start out by searing, and then I add my liquids. That way I get a nice look to the dish. You can also braise in the oven, which requires less attention and frees up some burners.

Dry-Heat Cooking

Dry-heat cooking methods, which are essential cooking techniques, include roasting, baking, broiling, grilling, and panfrying.

Roasting and Baking. When roasting and baking you're surrounding your dish with hot, dry air. That usually means an oven, although you could get the same result by making a fire in a pit in the ground. We discuss baking in the next chapter so focus on roasting here. Consider these roasting and baking tips:

↬ Rule number 1 for roasting: you do it *uncovered*. If you're covering it, then you're braising.

↬ When you roast something, you use a rack. Otherwise, it's sitting in—and simmering in—its own juice, which makes it moist-heat cooking, right?

↬ You'll get your best result when you roast if you rotate your dish a few times. That will make up for any unevenness in your oven.

Perfect Roast Chicken

The saying goes that a cook is only as good as his or her roast chicken. Certainly there are few dishes that can evoke such a feeling of comfort at the same time that they deserve a place on even the most sophisticated menu. There are many reliable techniques for producing a crisp, juicy, succulent roast chicken. We like the technique by fabled chef

---

Jacques Pépin. Keep in mind, however, that technique will only take you so far. The most important thing is to start with a really good bird, preferably a free-range chicken, widely available now, or a kosher chicken. You can experiment with other flavorings as well. Cumin, ginger, orange juice, garlic, lemon juice, and soy are popular options.

31/2 to 4 pound chicken
Salt and freshly ground pepper
3 tablespoons melted butter

Preheat oven to 400° to 425°. Season the cavity of the chicken and its exterior with the salt and pepper. Tie the legs together with chicken string, and slather the bird with the melted butter. Place chicken on its side on a rack in a roasting pan, bake 15 minutes, then turn it on its other side and bake 15 more minutes. Turn the chicken on its back, and baste well with the drippings. Bake another 25 to 35 minutes, basting frequently. When the leg joint wiggles easily, or when an instant-read thermometer inserted into the thigh reaches 165°, the bird is done. Let chicken rest 20 minutes before carving. If a natural gravy is desired, pour one-third cup of water into the pan five minutes before removing chicken from the oven to melt the solidified juices.

Broiling and Grilling

When broiling, you are using radiant heat from above. It is a rapid-cooking method, relying on very high heat, to be used primarily for tender meats, poultry, and fish. Certain vegetables, such as eggplant or zucchini, also lend themselves to this process. Grilling refers to cooking on an open grid over wood or charcoal, or on a gas grill. Here are some thoughts on broiling and grilling from those in the field:

✎ Broiling temperatures are either high or low. To adjust broiling, one adjusts the position of the rack and its proximity to the heat source, not the temperature itself.

✎ Preheating the broiler is very important. You want it hot, hot, hot.

✎ As a rule, one turn is all that is necessary.

✎ When broiling fish, you have to be really careful not to overcook it. Small slices or filets are best for broiling, and fatty fish, such as salmon, are better than lean fish.

✎ Paprika gives fish a nice color, but use it with a light hand. I've had fish served to me that tasted of nothing *but* paprika.

Sautéing and Panfrying

Whenever you see a chef at work in a movie, he or she always seems to be sautéing. It's a lively way to cook—very photogenic, with a lot of shaking and moving around. There is, however, a right way and a wrong way to go about it. Some tips from your culinary colleagues follow:

༄ Whatever you do, don't overcrowd your pan. It'll lower the temperature of the oil or butter, and your ingredients will wind up simmering instead of sautéing.

༄ A quick dredge in flour can make all the difference. If you're doing calves' livers, let's say, if you dust them with flour first, you'll get a much better browning when you sauté.

༄ You've got to preheat your pan before adding whatever it is you're sautéing. Searing works best when it happens fast.

The Favorite Sauté Pan

Different chefs favor different pans for sautéing, but many treasure the old spider—that black, cast-iron skillet you see selling for peanuts at tag sales. Sometimes they're horribly rusty and encrusted, but the fact is that a good spider is almost indestructible and can be rehabilitated easily. One way to deal with such a skillet is to stick it in a roaring fire, or put it through the self-cleaning cycle of an oven. When it cools, you can reseason it. Many chefs reseason their beloved spiders after each use. After cleaning, dry it on the range over high heat for up to five minutes. Then wipe the cooking surface with a tablespoon of oil. Occasional deep-frying in the skillet also will help keep it seasoned. These inexpensive pans are really superb.

✎ Panfrying is like sautéing, but you generally use a little more fat, and you have to count on the dish taking longer to cook.

Deep-Frying

Most people today do not relish the image of deep-frying. It looks dangerous and unhealthy. It needn't be either. Deep-frying is excellent for certain items, and crucial for others, such as French fries or doughnuts. It allows for the least fat absorption and the maximum crispiness. If you adhere to the following safety tips that we collected from your culinary colleagues you should encounter no problems with deep-frying:

✎ Remove any excess moisture from foods before you deep-fry. This minimizes spattering.

✎ Don't let any liquids sit around near a deep fryer. That can lead to accidents.

✎ Use a high-quality fat, and replenish with about 20 percent new fat after each use. Discard fat that's seen its day. Using fat over and over again will make your establishment smell like the proverbial greasy spoon.

✎ Make sure that you're doing your deep-frying at the correct temperatures. That generally means between 350° to 375°. Frying foods at temperatures that aren't high enough can lead to that yucky greasiness you want so much to avoid.

✎ Deep-fried foods need to be served very soon after they're prepared. They do not hold well.

Microwaving

The microwave obviously has played a revolutionary role in the modern kitchen. As these appliances become more and more sophisticated, they will become an ever-increasing presence in our lives. Some good tips follow to help you make the best use of them:

❧ As far as I'm concerned, the microwave is not the great white hope of a cook's life. In other words, you're not really going to *cook* with it. But it's a great kitchen appliance, the way a food processor is, for doing a variety of tasks.

❧ I'd say forget the microwave for most of what it's touted to do. Things like steaming broccoli or roasting squash are done so much better in or on a stove. Baked apples? No contest. They come out all wet in the microwave. There are, however, some things that the microwave does very well.

Some Good Things to Do with Your Microwave

Our poll of culinary professionals found the following microwave procedures most valuable:

❧ **Melting chocolate.** Great! You can melt four one-ounce squares at 50 percent power in a two-cup Pyrex™ dish in around 90 seconds. Then stir with a wooden spoon, and finish off until it's fully melted for another minute.

❧ Softening butter. Watch carefully, but it's a great shortcut as compared to letting the butter come to room temperature.

❧ Melting butter. The butter separates nicely, making it easier to clarify. Place a stick of butter, cut into eight pieces, in a two-cup Pyrex™ measuring cup, cover it loosely with plastic wrap, and microwave at 50 percent power until it's fully melted, two to two and a half minutes.

❧ Softening brown sugar. You know that rock-hard brown sugar problem? Here's an easy way to deal with it. Put your sugar in a glass pie plate, cover it with wax paper, pop a slice of bread on top to add some moisture, cover with plastic wrap, and nuke at 100 percent [power] for about 30 seconds.

❧ Warming eggs. Again, when you need room-temperature eggs, here's a good shortcut. Place an egg right from the fridge in a small bowl, and microwave at 30 percent power for 10 seconds.

❧ Warming up rice. So nice! Just sprinkle the rice with a few teaspoons of water, cover with vented plastic wrap, and microwave for about 90 seconds until the rice is soft and hot. Then let it stand for two minutes.

❧ Warming syrup. Warmed maple syrup on pancakes is just the kind of grace note that can give your establishment a special cachet. It's a snap in a microwave. Use a Pyrex™ cup of a microwaveable pitcher, and warm the syrup at full power for about 30 seconds.

A Few Shakes of Seasoning and a Dollop of Sauce

As we said at the top of this chapter, we only have room for a whirlwind tour through the world of cooking, and we can only offer the briefest overview of the basics of the kitchen. We'd hate to leave this chapter, however, without a word or two about seasoning and the use of sauces. These are the functions that make food come alive, and all culinary professionals need to develop a deft hand at them.

Seasoning

Imagine if salt was expensive. It would be one of the most valued things on earth. The same holds true for pepper, garlic, and other spices. Indeed, when certain spices were first introduced into the West from the East, they *were* among the most valued things on earth. Their value in cooking still cannot be overestimated. Let's hear what your fellow cooks have to say about seasoning.

✒ The most important thing is to familiarize yourself with the range of spices and herbs that are available. And I don't mean go to a chart and read about them. You need to use your nose and your taste buds to really explore what's out there and what the properties are of the different options. And there are always so many new options that come on the market. Years ago, for instance, who ever heard of garam masala or Chinese five-spice powder? Now they're all over the place.

✒ Buy spices on the high end. Really good quality is important here. Find a reliable and creative purveyor, and stay with him. And remember—you only use pinches here and there, so you can afford to pay a little more for quality.

✒ Be subtle with your seasoning. Aside from certain boldly spiced dishes like chilies or curries, you don't want your seasonings to be screaming out at you.

✒ Always make sure that your herbs and spices are very fresh. As a rule of thumb, they won't last more than six months. Store them away from heat, light, and moisture. They're quite fragile.

✒ When you use a fresh batch of spices or herbs, keep in mind that their flavor is more potent. You may need less. It's like opening a new can of tennis balls—there's a lot of bounce!

✒ Better to err on the side of less than more. Even though being timid with spices is a criticism often leveled at cooks, it's better to add than subtract.

✒ So many recipes end with the phrase "adjust seasoning." That means you should taste what you're cooking. Don't just slavishly follow a recipe. A recipe may say a half-teaspoon of freshly grated nutmeg, and, for whatever reason, you may just think it needs a bit more to make it fly. Go with it.

Sauces

Sauces work like seasonings: they enhance the experience of the dish. In the days of Escoffier, making sauces was the pinnacle of the chef's art. Today, it is commonplace for customers to shy away from sauces. Too many associate sauces with poorly made glop and are under the impression that they are very high in calories. A wonderful sauce on a dish, however, can be a revelation for even the most sauce-shy customer, and, of course, there's no need for sauces to be high in calories. Sauces add moisture, flavor, richness, and general appeal to a dish. They can still make a chef's name.

Whole books could be written on sauces and their preparations. We just "dip into" the topic with a look at "mother sauces," a term coined by nineteenth-century chef Antonin Carême, to refer to the four basic sauces. In general, sauces—not gravies—are liquids derived from stocks (a good subject for a whole other chapter) and thickened with such agents as *roux* (flour and oil cooked to a specific color), kneaded butter-flour (*beurre-manié*), heavy cream, such starches as cornstarch or arrowroot, tempered egg yolks, or pureed vegetables. The mother sauces follow:

✐ *Espagnole*. A rich brown sauce made from reduced brown stock with tomatoes and a *mirepoix* (roughly chopped mix) of vegetables, herbs, and seasonings, all thickened by a brown *roux*.

✐ *Velouté*. A white stock thickened with a white *roux*. The stock is usually made from chicken, veal, or fish.

✐ *Béchamel*. Milk thickened with a white *roux*.

> **Good Sauce Tip**
>
> Using a skillet instead of a Dutch oven will take considerable minutes off the time it takes to reduce and thicken a sauce. Switching from a large saucepan to a large skillet can cut out as much as five minutes of cooking time.

✒ *Allemande*. *Velouté* thickened with egg yolks.

Varying the mother sauces with added ingredients can produce other important sauces. For instance, hollandaise sauce features lemon along with egg yolks, while béarnaise sauce adds seasonings such as shallots and tarragon to the egg yolks.

Sauces are not things of the past. A contemporary adaptation of classic sauces can win you raves for your cooking, and there are countless sauces to be discovered and adapted from the world's great cuisines.

 *The Final Touches*

Customers usually are very pleased to get that little something "extra" at the end of the meal. Maybe it's a truffle or some other sweetmeat. We'd like to leave you with something "extra" in this chapter, so we've polled our culinary professionals regarding some of their favorite tips. Here's what they had to say:

✒ When measuring something viscous or sticky like honey or molasses, spray your measuring tool first with nonstick spray. The sticky stuff will slip right out. Anything left can be scraped out with a rubber spatula.

❧ Know your measurements! No matter what you're cooking, they always come up. Your job will be a lot easier if you know your measurements inside and out.

❧ Why put meat right onto a digital scale and then have to clean off the scale? Instead, slide the whole scale into a ziplock bag and then place the meat on that.

❧ When whipping cream, you want your bowl to be chilled. Here's how to get a bowl chilled fast: put ice cubes in a ziplock bag, and stick it in the bowl for a little while. You could use frozen freezer packs too.

❧ A high-quality nonstick skillet is an expensive item and can be damaged easily with scratches and nicks. Store the skillet between sheets of bubblewrap or between shirt cardboards.

❧ Preparation is everything. When juicing citrus, roll the fruit first, and then cut it on the extreme bias for maximum juice output. When using fresh herbs for hot food preparation, add them at the end for maximum flavor, just like salt and pepper. You have to know these tricks of the trade.

❧ Warm dinner plates are a gracious touch. Even in the smallest kitchen, you can offer this by warming the plates on the dry cycle of the dishwasher.

❧ Pound for pound, nuts are some of the most expensive ingredients you'll be using. Store your nuts in the freezer. It's ideal.

❧ Some of our desserts utilize ice cream in a̶ [la] *mode* presentation. It's a hassle to scoop it from̶ for this purpose, so we freeze scoops of ice crea̶m ahead of time and put them, wrapped with plastic wrap, in paper-lined muffin tins in the freezer.

❧ Debone salmon by placing the fish on top of an aluminum bowl. The curvature causes the pin bones to pop out.

❧ After cutting onions, garlic, or fish, you can use lemon juice to wipe your hands. Mouthwash also works well to take away the odor.

❧ Is your lettuce wilted? You can revive it or other greens by putting them in an ice water bath for 10 minutes.

❧ Sometimes you'll let some specks of egg yolk escape into the egg whites you're planning to whip. I use a cotton swab to get them out.

❧ Pan measurements always refer to [the] top diameter of the pan, from the outside rim to the outside rim. It's just a good thing to be clear about.

❧ I find that placing a dish towel over rice or mashed potatoes in a pot will absorb water beautifully. Just make sure the towel ends don't catch [on] fire.

❧ Dotting something with butter can be a real pain. Use a vegetable peeler with frozen butter—it's painless!

❧ Did you ever hull a strawberry by pushing a drinking straw through it? It works.

↝ Waste not, want not. I save lemon shells to use for acidulated water.

↝ A great way to get salad greens really dry is to spin them with a sheet of paper towel.

. . . And a Few Great Inventions

In closing, we want to mention several truly marvelous, revolutionary kitchen tools that have been introduced in recent years. They are guaranteed to change your life.

One of the most onerous chores in the kitchen is grating lemon and orange rinds. Then along came the Microplane®, discovered in Canada by the resourceful wife of a hardware store owner in a desperate moment while baking an orange cake. The Microplane®, which is essentially a wood rasp, has hundreds of tiny, very sharp teeth. It makes short—almost miraculous—work of grating citrus rind, hard cheeses, chocolate, garlic, carrots, radishes, and whole nutmegs. It is also cheap and a snap to clean. In other words, absolutely indispensable.

The OXO™ vegetable peeler (and OXO™ products in general) is another revelation. The soft, rubberized handles allow you to apply a great deal of pressure when peeling without any discomfort to your hand. Again, it makes short order of all peeling tasks. It's an ergonomic wonder.

A third wonder is the Silpat™ mat, which was developed in France in 1982. Made of a silicone-coated fiberglass mesh, the mat can be used over and over again in place of parchment paper. You don't have to be involved with cutting anything to size. Simply lay the mat on the baking sheet and go. Nothing will stick to it. You can bake your cookies on it (even macaroons or meringues), you can roll out pie dough on it, and you can use it up to 500°.

We now move on to specialties, starting with baking in the next chapter.

Mayonnaise

Mayonnaise is an indispensable dressing. For most people that means opening up a jar, and we have to say that Hellman's™ is a product that you can reliably turn to for a host of needs. From-scratch mayonnaise is, however, a classic preparation with which every cook should be familiar.

Mayonnaise is a permanent-emulsion dressing. Oil and vinegar do not naturally come together. When they are made to, thus forming a uniform mixture, we call that an *emulsion*, and we say that one liquid is in *suspension* in the other. The egg yolk in the mayonnaise is the emulsifying agent.

Some guidelines in terms of ingredients: use the freshest eggs possible; have all ingredients at room temperature; and, most important, add the oil very slowly at first. Now, for the actual procedure:

8 egg yolks
6 tablespoons vinegar

2 teaspoons salt
2 teaspoons dry mustard
a pinch of cayenne pepper
7 cups salad oil (a neutral oil such as corn is fine)
3 to 4 tablespoons lemon juice

- Place the egg yolks in the bowl of an electric mixer, and beat well with the whip attachment.
- Add two tablespoons of the vinegar, and beat well.
- Mix the dry ingredients, and add them to the bowl. Beat well.
- Turn the mixer to the highest speed. *Very slowly*, add the oil, almost drop by drop. When you see the emulsion forming, you can begin to cautiously add the oil a little faster.
- When the mayonnaise becomes thickened, thin it out with a bit of the remaining vinegar. Gradually beat in the remaining oil alternately with the rest of the vinegar.
- Adjust the tartness and consistency by beating in the lemon juice a little at a time, tasting as you go along.

Chapter 10

On the Rise

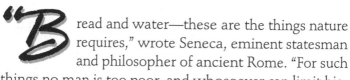

"**B**read and water—these are the things nature requires," wrote Seneca, eminent statesman and philosopher of ancient Rome. "For such things no man is too poor, and whosoever can limit his desire to them alone can rival Jupiter for happiness."

For thousands of years—some say as long as *8,000 years*—bread has played an enormously significant role in the human experience. Christians pray for their "daily bread." Jews utilize *matzoh*—the bread of affliction—as one of their primary religious symbols. Muslim brides must eat 21 small *chapatis* before leaving the wedding. We speak of "bread" and "dough" as slang for money. In addition, all kinds of superstitions have arisen around bread through the ages. Make a cross on your dough to let the devil out. Cut bread at both ends and the devil will fly over the house. Leave bread and coffee under a house to prevent ghosts from calling. Once upon a time, sailors took hot cross buns to sea to ward off shipwrecks.

What explains this great fascination that bread holds for us all? It comes, to some extent, from the fact that it is a cheap and delicious way to fill ourselves up. James Beard, dean of American food writers, wrote: "Good bread is the most fundamentally satisfying of all foods; and good bread with fresh butter, the greatest of feasts." Baking, in general, is the great love of many in the culinary field because it gives so much pleasure. Cakes and cookies, muffins and scones, and pies and tarts make people happy, and when you make people happy, it's hard not to be happy yourself. The creativity of baking is another thing that lures people into this field. Creating a dazzling wedding cake or being asked to make a cake that looks like the Sydney Opera House or the White House is a great challenge, and pulling it off is a great thrill to the professional baker.

In this chapter, we look at the fundamentals of baking, with far more than a "baker's dozen" of helpful hints.

The Science of Bread Making

We begin our discussion by going right to the heart of the matter: yeasted breads. For the master baker, that's what it's all about. That's where the real art is, and interested bakers have been known to travel all over the world looking for the perfect formula to make the perfect bread.

Let's see how your fellow bakers understand the process of baking.

❧ The science of it is pretty simple. Bread rises because gas—carbon dioxide (CO_2)—is produced by the yeast and gets trapped in the dough. The more gas that's released, the more space it needs—this is basic physics, right?—and so the more the dough is pushed up and out. That's called "rising." When you bake the bread, what you're essentially doing is killing off the yeast and putting an end to the production of the gas.

❧ We talk of dough as being elastic. It needs to stretch. The ingredient that allows the dough to stretch is the gluten in the flour. That's why you need strong bread flours with high levels of gluten.

❧ The carbon dioxide is produced by fermentation. When we use active yeast and we mix it into dough with a warm liquid, we're giving the yeast all the basic life support it needs. We're giving it food (the sugar or starch in the dough), moisture (liquid), and warmth (a warm rising place).

❧ Your yeast mixture needs to be handled with care. Any extremes of temperature can damage it. Very cold conditions will leave it sitting there, twiddling its thumbs, and very hot conditions will destroy it. The optimal temperatures for yeast development are between 70°F and 90°F (21°–32C°) for fresh yeast, 105°F and 115°F (41°–46C°) for dry yeast, and 125°F to 130°F (52°–54C°) for activating instant yeast.

✎ The microwave is a good place to proof bread. You can cut your rising time by up to 20 minutes. Here's what you do: Microwave two cups of water to boil at 100 percent power in a one-quart Pyrex™ measuring cup. Alongside the water, place your bowl of dough, covered with plastic wrap. Close the microwave door, and let the dough stand until it doubles in size.

✎ Once your bread dough has been mixed and kneaded, you can refrigerate it for up to five days. You can also store dough in the freezer for up to three months, but once you thaw it, you shouldn't keep it at room temperature for more than two hours.

Flour

Bread is only as good as the flour that you use to make it. Your fellow bakers have some interesting things to say on the topic of flour.

✎ I personally always prefer using some form of whole grain flour. It doesn't have to be exclusively whole grain, but I love mixing whole grains into white flours. Whole wheat flours can become rancid, however, so you have to take care when it comes to storing them. I store them in the refrigerator.

✎ I like to use whole wheat flours, but I always look for more of a rise on them. Adding some white flour helps, but I also learned from another baker that you can add a half teaspoon of Vitamin C powder, which you can get at a pharmacy, to the mix.

✎ Some people are confused about the difference between bread flour and cake flour. Bread flour is a strong flour—"strong" meaning high in protein (gluten). Cake flour is a weak, or low-gluten, flour that has a very soft, downy texture and a pure white color. Pastry flour falls in-between. It's creamy white, like bread dough, but is lower in gluten than bread dough. Pastry dough is used for cookies, pie pastry, biscuits, and muffins.

✐ I often get asked by the layman if you really have to sift your flour prior to using it. Many flours come presifted, and if you're mixing your ingredients with a wire whisk, you can probably get away without sifting, but I usually sift anyway. Sifting is especially important with cakes and batters.

Yeast

This magical and mysterious organism can intimidate novice bakers. Your fellow bakers offer some helpful hints on the yeast front.

✐ It's important to understand the difference between active dried yeast, which is compressed yeast, and what is referred to as "rapid rise" yeast. Active dried yeast has had its moisture removed and needs to be reactivated with water before being used. The rapid rise yeast is a combination of dried yeast to which Vitamin C (ascorbic acid) has been added.

✐ You should always take the time to "proof" your yeast. That means activating the yeast by adding a little water and sugar to make sure that the yeast is still viable. What's the point of going through all the trouble of preparing dough if you don't have viable yeast?

. . . And a Few Words about Other Important Ingredients

Flour and yeast are your mainstays, but other ingredients come into play.

Baking soda. This is the chemical compound sodium bicarbonate. Acids present in substances such as honey, buttermilk, fruit juice, molasses, or chocolate react with the soda to release carbon dioxide gas, which leavens the batter. Heat is not necessary but the batter must be baked at once to take advantage of the leavening.

Baking powder. This compound is a mix of baking soda with the acids necessary to react with it. Single-acting baking powder only requires moisture to release the gas. Double-acting baking powder releases some gas when it's cold but requires heat for the complete reaction. Excess baking powder will create an "off" taste, so be careful when using it. Also, keep in mind that baking powder has a finite shelf life.

I always add salt when I'm working with yeast, because not only will it improve the taste of the final product, but also it will keep the yeast from veering out of control. And yet too much salt can actually retard the development of the yeast, so you want to make sure you have a buffer zone of flour between the salt and the yeast.

🌱 Store yeast in a cool, dry, dark place in an airtight container. You can also store it in the refrigerator, where it will keep longer than indicated by the expiration date printed on the packet. You can even keep it in the freezer for up to a year. If you bake a lot, it makes good economic sense to buy yeast in large amounts and keep it in the freezer. Stick it in a tightly sealed, plastic container, mark the date, and return it to room temperature before you use it.

🌱 When I place dough in a bowl to rise, I use non-stick spray to grease the inside of the bowl, and I give a spritz of the spray to the dough itself. It's a nice, neat way to handle it.

🌱 A good way to keep track of your dough rise is to mark the outside of the bowl that you place the dough in with a rubber band. It's a quick visual aid when you go to check on its status.

Troubleshooting Bread Problems

The basic process of making bread is a fairly simple one once you get the hang of it. But things *can* go wrong. Here are some yeasty tips from the bakers that we spoke with:

🌱 Sometimes your dough will rise, but then when you go to bake it, it kind of collapses in the middle. The problem was that you allowed the dough to become too light during its preparation, and it rose too much. It became a little like a soufflé instead of a bread dough. If the bread collapses only in the middle, it probably means that you introduced too much liquid into the dough.

❧ If your dough refuses to rise, it may be that your yeast is outdated. Check the package. It may also mean that your rising place wasn't warm enough. Also, the temperature of the water you used to activate the yeast could be the culprit. If it was too cold, it wouldn't have activated the yeast. If it was too warm, it might have killed the yeast.

❧ If you find a big crack along the top of your bread, it probably means that the dough wasn't mixed well enough, or that it was too stiff. A crack along the side might indicate an unevenness in the oven temperature, or an insufficient rising period. You could experiment with different-shaped loaves to see if you have better luck with them.

❧ I've had breads that looked lovely when I took them out of the oven and then just went and crumbled on me. I was told the problem could be traced back to one or more factors. Maybe I didn't mix the ingredients well enough. I might have added too much flour to the dough. Maybe I left it to rise too long or in too warm a place, or maybe the oven wasn't hot enough. Very frustrating after all that work . . .

❧ A few times my loaves smelled all yeasty and had a sour taste. And they weren't sourdough breads. What happened is that I let them rise too long, or maybe the rising place was too warm.

❧ A dry, heavy bread suggests that you put in too much flour, or maybe you didn't knead the dough long enough. Having the oven temperature set too low could also cause this problem. If the bread is wet inside, you probably had too short a rising period.

෴ Sometimes you get a loaf with bagel-sized holes in it. That's because the dough rose for too long before baking, or the air wasn't totally squeezed out of it when you shaped the loaves.

෴ If you're cooking breads in tins, make sure you remove them after baking so that they can sit on a wire rack to cool. If not, you'll get a yucky, doughy bottom.

෴ Those artisanal loaves you see all over the place now are beautiful, but hard to slice. Slice them sideways. It makes it much easier.

Measuring Ingredients

Always use the dip 'n sweep method when measuring dry ingredients such as flour, sugar, baking powder, and baking soda. Dip the measuring cup or spoon into the dry ingredient, and then level it off with a knife. This is the most accurate method of measurement.

Egg Wash

Certain bread recipes will call for an egg wash, in which egg and water are mixed and then brushed on top of a loaf to give it shine and color, as in a challah. To just get the shine without the color, make a wash of two parts egg white to one part vegetable oil.

Muffins and Scones (and the Occasional Biscuit)

Muffins and scones, which have become omnipresent in recent years, are related to quick breads (e.g., banana bread, date-nut bread). These breads wow customers wherever they're served. They obviously require a lot less labor than yeasted breads do, so they are a good option for small restaurants and shops.

Muffins

A great place to go creative! Blueberries, cornmeal, whole corn kernels, raspberries, cranberries, walnuts, cheddar cheese, pumpkin, bran, granola, carrot . . . there's no end. Let's hear what your fellow bakers have to say on the subject.

✎ Always mix your dry ingredients and your wet ingredients separately. That way the combining takes the least amount of time, and you don't run the risk of overmixing, which can lead to a tough muffin.

✎ Make a well in your dry ingredients, and pour your wet ingredients into the well. Then mix. Don't worry about a few lumps. It's perfectly okay to have lumps in muffin batter.

✎ Don't agitate about not overfilling the muffin cups. Nothing terrible will happen. You'll get a big muffin, which certainly is not going to bother anyone.

✐ Muffin tops are cool and sell like hotcakes, if you don't mind the mixed metaphor. There are special pans for making them.

✐ Whenever I make muffins, I use buttermilk in place of regular milk, no matter what the recipe says. Buttermilk lends a special moistness and flavor to the muffins. Fresh buttermilk is great, but the dry powdered buttermilk works well too.

✐ If you really want to make a memorable muffin, grease your pans or use a nonstick muffin pan. Muffin tins and paper cups are convenient in terms of cleanup, to be sure, but they don't make as good a muffin. The bottoms can get soggy, or you can lose some of your muffin if it adheres to the liner.

✐ If you've miscalculated and run short on the batter, and you've got empty places in your muffin tin that you've already greased, put a little water in those empty places so the grease doesn't scorch.

✐ Peaks and tunnels in muffins are usually caused by overmixing. Remember to love your lumps and to stir only until just moistened.

✐ Always bake to the minimum amount of baking time. Overdone muffins lose a lot of their appeal. Check the muffins regularly as they cook. When the tops are nice and golden, they're done . . . no matter how long your recipe tells you to cook them.

✐ Do muffin ledges disturb you? (They're those usually unwanted rims around the edge of your muffin).

If so, try greasing the muffin cups only on the bottoms and just halfway up the sides.

❧ To freeze muffins, let them completely cool to room temperature. Then wrap each one separately in foil, place in freezer bags, and stick them in the freezer, where they'll be good for up to two months.

Scones

Once upon a time, scones were the companion of crumpets and were found almost exclusively in the United Kingdom, where they were served with Devonshire cream and strawberry preserves. Now scones are found in every other luncheonette and take-out shop in America. Why not? They're jolly good!

❧ Sometimes you'll make a scone that comes out heavy. Try cutting the butter or other fat into the dry ingredients a little beyond the coarse-crumb stage that most recipes call for.

❧ As with muffins, stir just until moistened. Don't overmix.

❧ Unlike muffins, scones require a little kneading. Do it gently, or you may wind up with a dry, tough crumb.

❧ A hard crust on a scone is probably the fault of an uneven oven temperature. Verify your temperature with an oven thermometer if you expect that it's the culprit.

And Don't Forget Biscuits

Biscuits are not that often seen today, but the homey touch they lend to a menu delights patrons. As with muffins and scones, beware of overmixing and overkneading. Using slightly less shortening and cutting it into the dry ingredients somewhat less than called for will produce a flakier biscuit. Dispensing with the kneading step of biscuit making will produce an extremely tender and crusty but fragile biscuit.

How Sweet It Is

We are now ready to move into the big baking payoff—the sweet stuff. Cakes, cookies, brownies, pies . . . isn't that what life is all about?

Cakes

Obviously, whole books—*many* whole books—are written on the subject of cakes and assorted pastries, including devil's food cake, pound cake, chiffon cake, angel food cake, wedding cake . . . we could go on and on. We only have room, however, to offer a few good general tips from fellow bakers on the time-honored art of baking cakes.

✐ Rule number 1: Preheat your oven, or your precious cake will never rise!

Overmixing the cake batter will cause tunnels in your cake. And who wants tunnels in a cake when you could have cake instead? Mix your ingredients until they're just combined. If the oven temperature is too high, that could cause tunneling too.

 When creaming butter, it can take a long time for the stick of chilled butter to come to the right temperature for creaming. If you're in a hurry—and who isn't?—you can speed up the softening process by cutting the butter into tablespoon-sized pieces. This will gain you almost 15 minutes of softening time. If you start creaming and discover that your butter is still too cool, it will look shiny and granular after you add the sugar rather than thick, dull, and smooth like you want it to be. What you need to do is to wrap your mixing bowl with a warm damp towel and proceed.

 To make sure your cake doesn't come out heavy and compact, stir your flour and baking powder before scooping and leveling. This leads to precise measuring, which is really critical when it comes to baking cakes.

 If you're working in a small kitchen, or in a home kitchen if you have a catering business, here's a good trick when it comes to keeping track of how many eggs you've used in a cake: as you crack the eggs, put the shells in the individual compartments of the egg carton. I can't tell you how many times I lost track of my egg count before I learned this trick. Similarly, you should spread out a sheet of waxed paper or parchment and make little mounds of all your dry ingredients like baking powder, salt, soda, cinnamon, and so on. That's another visual way of seeing what you've used so far, in case you lose track.

✑ When making an angel food, sponge, or chiffon cake, beat the egg whites until stiff peaks form. If you notice any large, trapped air bubbles running through the batter, break them up with a rubber spatula. Don't knock the pan against the counter to do this, because that will reduce the much-valued volume of these cakes. Sponge cakes can be nicely cooled by inverting them over a wine bottle.

✑ What explains the sad end of a fallen cake? Well, it could be that your oven wasn't hot enough, or maybe it was too hot at the start of the baking. Did you over-mix? Did you not leave your cake in long enough? Did you keep opening the oven door to check on it? Too much of certain things—too much flour or sugar or leavening—can be the reason too.

✑ If your cake came out dry, you probably overbaked it, or maybe you overbeat the egg whites or added too much flour or leavening or didn't add enough shortening or sugar. Does that help?

✑ Cakes that crack or fall apart have generally been removed from the pan too soon.

✑ If your cake has a sticky texture, you probably didn't bake it long enough. Sorry. Or maybe the oven wasn't hot enough.

✑ Place your cake on a lazy Susan to ice it. It's a neat trick. Anchoring the bottom layer with a dab of frosting also works wonders.

✐ Did you know that frosted cakes stay fresh longer than unfrosted ones? Think of the frosting as insulation.

✐ Cool cakes completely before frosting them. Elementary, my dear Watson.

✐ Baker's Joy™ is a wonderful product to discover. It makes greasing and flouring cake pans into a one-step process. Dried egg whites are also a nice convenience ingredient to have around.

✐ To prevent nuts and fruits from sinking to the bottom of a cake during baking, try warming them a little in the oven and tossing them with flour. Shake off the excess flour before incorporating them into the cake batter. Should work!

✐ I find I get my best results if I let my basic ingredients—eggs, butter, and milk—come to room temperature before mixing them.

✐ Did you ever have this problem where your icing is running off your cake? Here's a cool tip. Dust the cake with cornstarch first. It will give the icing a little traction without affecting the taste or the appearance.

✐ When a cake recipe calls for flouring the baking pan, use a bit of your dry cake mix. It'll all blend in nicely, rather than showing white flour on the end product. Try dusting pans for dark-colored cakes with cocoa.

Pies and Tarts

Mmm . . . may I have another slice of that pie, please? Pies are instant gratification. Everybody loves them—you *must* have them on your menu—but unfortunately not everyone makes them well. A pie is a baked crust with a sweet or savory filling. It can be an open-faced (without a top crust), a double-crusted, or a lattice-topped pie. A tart is like a pie but is made in a shallow, straight-edged pan that often has fluted edges. Some hints from your fellow bakers on the subject of pies and tarts follow:

⚬ If your crusts have been soggy, try brushing the bottom of the crust with egg white before adding your fruit. A soggy crust can also come about if your oven temperature is too low.

⚬ To avoid burnt edges on your crust, either use pie shields or, if you don't have them, you can take a foil pie plate, cut out the center, and use the rim as a pie shield.

⚬ A shrinking crust means you overmixed or over-worked the dough. It could also mean you didn't have enough fat in the dough, so you'll have to adjust your formula.

⚬ With a custard filling, if it "weeps" or separates, that means you've probably put in too many eggs, or that the eggs are overcooked.

⚬ Always chill your pastry dough thoroughly before rolling and cutting it. Then chill it again before baking it to relax the gluten even further.

⚬ For a double-crusted pie, brush a little water around the edges of the bottom crust before you put on the top crust. The water will create a nice seal when the two are crimped together.

ᴥ Have you ever tried baking a pie on a pizza stone? It helps to absorb excess moisture, and if you've got a pie tin with some holes punched into it, you'll get a super-crispy outcome.

ᴥ Here's a good trick. Brush beaten egg white over the crust before you bake it. You'll get this glossy finish that'll have people oohing and aahing.

ᴥ For a flakier upper crust, try brushing a little cold water all over it before you put it in the oven.

ᴥ This is what I do with a pumpkin pie or any kind of custard pies. I break one of the eggs called for by the pie filling right into the unbaked pastry shell, and I whoosh it around so that the egg white covers the entire surface. This prevents sogginess.

ᴥ If you're worried about your meringue shrinking, spread it on the pie while the filling is still hot. Also, make sure to stretch the meringue out to the edges of the crust, all around.

ᴥ One way to prevent a sticky meringue is to add a pinch of cream of tartar to the egg whites before beating. The meringue won't stick to your knife when you cut the pie if you've done that.

ᴥ I don't know where I heard this idea, but it's really worked well for me. When I blind-bake pastry crust, instead of using dried beans or pie weights to weigh it down, I have a 30-inch stainless steel choke dog collar that I lay in the crust. It works great. Just don't use it on your dog in-between!

❧ Here's a trick I've learned about how to remove a tart from its ring. Lower it over an aluminum can.

Cookies

One of life's great simple pleasures, cookies come in an endless variety of shapes, sizes, textures, and tastes. Certain overriding rules, however, apply across the board to cookies. Let's listen to our culinary professionals share their thoughts:

❧ Cookies made with butter tend to spread out, because the butter spreads out as it melts. Cookies made with oil, which is already a liquid at room temperature, hold their shapes better.

❧ The amount of fat in a cookie is an important factor in a cookie's outcome. The more fat you use, the flatter, chewier, and crisper the cookie will be. Less fat creates a puffier, more cakelike cookie.

❧ Use unbleached all-purpose flour for your cookies. Cake flour will produce too cakey a cookie.

❧ Baking powder produces a lighter-colored, puffier cookie than baking soda does.

❧ White sugar makes a crispier cookie than brown sugar. Cookies made with brown sugar absorb moisture and stay chewier longer. If you use less sugar than a recipe calls for, you'll get a puffier cookie.

❧ For chewy cookies, remove them from the oven while their centers are still soft and not quite cooked all the way through. Using egg yolks instead of whole eggs also makes a chewier cookie. Reducing the amount of leavening—baking soda or baking powder—will also create more chewiness.

✑ If you like cookies really crisp, cook them a little extra . . . but not to the point of burning them! Use all butter and a high amount of sugar, and bake in the lower third of the oven.

✑ Adding a tablespoon or two of water or other liquid to your batter will make cookies spread and become flatter and crisper.

✑ When using cookie cutters, dip the cutter into flour each time before making your cuts. That way the dough won't adhere to the cutter. Work with small amounts of dough at a time, and keep the unused portions refrigerated until you're ready to cut out more snowmen or seashells or whatever.

✑ Everybody loves biscotti these days. A great shortcut is to bake biscotti on a wire rack set on a cookie sheet. That way, when you're drying them out in their second baking, you don't have to turn them over to do 10 minutes per side.

✑ Parchment paper is great, but don't forget about those amazing Silpat™ mats. Nothing beats them for baking.

✑ Cookie dough freezes extremely well, so consider that as an option. Keep in mind, however, that the dough will absorb odors like a sponge, so wrap it in double layers and date it. When you're ready to bake it, just let it defrost in the refrigerator for a few hours.

Beautiful Brownies

People often call jazz the great American indigenous art form, but we'd say that brownies are a close second. They've become a must-have on buffet tables, at take-home food shops, in boxed lunches . . . wherever their neat sweetness is desired. Some tips for brownie success follow:

🌀 Always hand mix your brownies. Don't use a beater.

🌀 Never overbake. It will create a dry and unpopular product.

🌀 Use the right pan size for the recipe. Altering the pan size will alter the texture of the brownie, giving you a chewy one where you might prefer a cakey one.

🌀 For no-clean-up brownies, line the brownie pan with aluminum foil. The cooled brownies will simply lift out and can be easily cut into squares.

🌀 Cool brownies completely before cutting, or they will crumble.

Already-baked cookies can also be frozen successfully and will keep for three to four weeks.

. . . And a Few Odds and Ends

We leave this chapter now, although we could go on and on talking about quiche and pizza and what have you. But we don't want to leave without sharing just a few more valuable hints from your culinary colleagues about the ingredients you'll be using.

✺ Always use whole milk in your pastry recipes. Skimping with low-fat or skim milk just won't work. Pastry dough is not the place to save calories!

✺ Bring your eggs to room temperature before using them, unless you're separating eggs. It's easier to separate an egg when it's cold.

✺ Always keep chocolate at room temperature. Cold chocolate is unpredictable and hard to work with. It will splinter and fly around.

✺ White chocolate has to be melted over very hot water—not boiling water or even simmering water. It will scorch at a much lower temperature than dark chocolate.

✺ Sometimes you'll see a grayish coating on your chocolate. That's called a "bloom," and you should know that it's completely harmless. It won't affect the flavor. It only happens because the cocoa butter has risen to the surface.

✺ I like to maximize the flavor of nuts by toasting them a bit before I incorporate them into a recipe. Given how expensive they can be, you really do want to maximize their impact.

Okay, as much as we hate to, we have to pull ourselves out of the bakery right now. Onward to some of the more specialized—and fascinating—realms of the culinary professional.

Chapter Reference

Beard, James (1973). *Beard on bread*. New York: Alfred A. Kropf.

Seneca quote accessed April 2, 2004, at Flour Advisory Board, www.fabflour.co.uk.

Stir-Fry

An important aspect of being involved in the food world is maintaining an interest in and an openness to new ways of cooking, new ingredients, and new preparations from cuisines around the world. This might be the year that you discover *panka*, marvelous Japanese bread crumbs that will lend your fried foods a special lightness, or piquillo peppers from Spain, which come jarred or bottled and are ideal for a range of stuffings.

Quite some time ago, stir-frying was introduced to many American kitchens. Now it is fairly standard, but let's not forget how useful it is. It is a healthy, fast way of cooking, and the procedure that follows will let you know whether or not you are doing it correctly.

- Heat a work or sauté pan over high heat until it is very hot.
- Add a small amount of oil, and allow it to heat.
- Flavor the oil with seasonings, depending on your recipe. Garlic, ginger, and scallions are typical flavoring agents in Asian recipes.

- If using meat, poultry, or seafood in the dish, add them now, making sure not to overload the pan. Allow these ingredients to sit untouched for a few moments to brown. Then stir them and toss with a spatula, searing evenly.

- If using any liquid ingredients such as soy sauce to flavor the meat, poultry, or seafood, add them now. Use only small amounts so the searing can continue.

- Depending on the recipe you are following, remove the items just mentioned or leave them in, and add the vegetables. (Usually, if quick-cooking vegetables such as spinach or watercress are used, the meat, poultry, or seafood items will not have to be removed.)

- Add a little more oil and refresh with the seasonings you have been using.

- Add the vegetables to the pan, and stir-fry, beginning with vegetables that take the longest to cook.

- Add any other liquid items to finish cooking the vegetables, such as stock or water, and stir often.

- Return the meat, poultry, or seafood, and finish the cooking. Often at this point a mixture of cornstarch and water will be added to thicken the sauce. Consult your recipe.

- Serve at once.

Chapter 11

A Range of Opportunities

One of the great things about becoming a culinary professional is that it gives you skills that you can take with you wherever you go. People will always be interested in the dining experience, and those professionals who know how to prepare delicious food can expect to find themselves in demand. The question becomes, which position in the field suits you best? Do you want to be a *chef de cuisine*, ultimately working your way up to a chef-owner? Or do you want to be a demonstration chef, working on TV, in stores, or for a food manufacturer? How does a corporate chef sound, serving power luncheons in beautifully appointed private dining rooms? Or perhaps you'd prefer to be a caterer, pulling together lavish affairs at exotic and luxurious venues?

Think about all of the places culinary professionals can be employed—on a yacht, at a country club, at an inn, in a school, in a retirement community, in a supermarket, in a test kitchen, at a spa, in a hospital. To decide which situation would work best, consider the various aspects of each to determine their importance to you. Is job security your number-one goal? Is creativity the thing that races your motor? Do you like to be with people, or are you more of a solitary traveler? Do you enjoy being around children, or do they make you break out in hives? Do you want to travel? Are you entrepreneurial?

In this chapter, we explore the range of opportunities for culinary professionals and hear interesting tips and insights from those who work within these different niches. We begin with one of the most important avenues of opportunity for the culinary professional: catering.

The Catered Affair

A lot of culinary professionals who go into catering do so because they feel that it's the ultimate in glamour. Owning your own restaurant is obviously quite glamorous too, but who gets to see more high-wattage stars than the lucky caterer who does fancy affairs? In fact, what about becoming a caterer who provides the food on movie sets? If you watch the long list of credits at the end of a feature film, the caterer is always mentioned. Wouldn't it be a blast to spend your days and nights serving meals to movie stars?

Hold on, dreamer. Behind every beautiful fantasy is a dark—or at least a less beautiful—reality. Caterers to movie stars have to endure the same problems, or worse, as everyone else. They still have to deal with wholesalers, schedules, and crises, and that sort of thing tends to take away from the joy of it all. Not that you won't necessarily like being a caterer to the stars, but to decide where best to put your talents, you really need to understand what you're getting into. We hear next the unvarnished truth from your fellow professionals who have gone into the catering business.

✎ The best thing about it? It's entrepreneurial. The worst thing about it? It's entrepreneurial. Any business where you're working for yourself comes with enormous highs and stomach-churning lows. In other words, it's a roller coaster, so hang on.

✎ Being a caterer is so *not* about hobnobbing with movie stars and jet-setters at fancy openings. Those people couldn't care less about you; you're just the poor schnook who brings out the food. The real reason to go into catering is because you've got a dramatic flair for food that can match the dramatic intensity of a big event. Now that's a talent!

✎ It can get pretty dicey starting a catering business, because you might tell yourself, "Oh, I'll just have a little sideline business while my husband (or wife), the gastroenterologist, is raking in the big bucks." But then, if you're good, you start getting calls, and suddenly that little sideline business can become a totally consuming enterprise that has you sweating bullets with knots in your stomach half the time. Controlling the part-time/full-time thing can be very difficult.

❧ Again, it's all about measuring the fantasy against the reality. I went into the catering business thinking I was going to be doing beautiful events, and I wound up doing weddings with swans made out of chopped liver. Not so much fun . . .

❧ You might go into the catering business thinking that you're going to like being a sole practitioner, but then you realize that you really need a partner. To be working on your own as a caterer means that you have to be good at everything: organizing, client contact, menu preparation, and—let's not forget—cooking. Most of us are not so good at everything, so joining forces with someone whose skills complement your own can be a good idea. Or a bad one—depending on the person. You really have to know a person *very* well to enter into a business partnership with him or her. And then only do it with the advice of your attorney. You can't imagine how sticky business partnerships can get.

❧ The good thing about it is that if you're catering from home, you have almost no overhead—the gas or electricity from your oven, your water, if you pay for it, the wear and tear on your appliances. You don't need to take out a second mortgage to get going, or to sink a lot of money into your business and put yourself into a terrifying money crunch.

❧ There are great perks to catering. You can buy your family's food at the same wholesale prices that you buy the food for your jobs. And there are often leftovers.

🖎 It's a pretty consuming business. Don't even think about "doing it all." Get help. You'll probably need to get a cleaning person in to take care of the home front. Or else you're going to have to become very immune to dust balls.

🖎 Guess what? I started losing weight when I went into catering. That napoleon that I could drool over is not so appetizing when you've got 100 of them lined up. Most nights, after catering, all I want is a piece of toast and a cup of tea.

The Many Sides of Catering

The field we call "catering" actually has a number of distinct paths from which you can choose. Let's get the scoop from those culinary professionals who have chosen this direction:

🖎 I am a full-service caterer. That means that if you [have], or your firm has, a need, I can meet it. I can do breakfast, lunch, dinner, afternoon tea, dessert parties, cocktail parties, and I can bring as much staff as is necessary to serve at any of those functions.

🖎 Don't even think about calling yourself a full-service caterer if you aren't one. A full-service caterer will be able to provide the tableware, the linens, the balloons, the flowers, the Gypsy violinists, and in many cases will even locate the venue for the event. That's why full-service catering is so exciting, so hard, and so insane!

ᕙ I started out thinking I was going to do full-service catering, and after a few truly horrible experiences, I scaled back and now I do what's called "no-service" catering. That means I prepare and deliver the food . . . that's it. I specialize in dinners for busy professional couples. I have a very loyal clientele, and I know that Mr. Jones hates anchovies, Mrs. Jones doesn't like curry, and the little Joneses are happy with chicken fingers for every meal. It's funny that I call what I do "no-service catering," because what I'm really doing is providing the highest level of personal service, but the term literally means that I don't have to think about providing a waitstaff.

ᕙ When I started out, I did what's called "partial-service" catering. I went to people's apartments and made dinner parties and stuff. Usually I brought along a friend and we served the meal together. I wound up eventually going into a retail operation—I own a muffin shop now—but I can legitimately say that I used to be in catering.

ᕙ Until five years ago, I was almost exclusively in social catering, which is what you call it when you're doing weddings, bar mitzvahs, graduations, and all those other life passages. I had an okay time with it for a while anyway, but ultimately I decided to go into corporate catering. People will tell you how wonderful it is to share the joy of weddings and all that, but do you know how much craziness comes out around weddings and bar mitzvahs and stuff? Unbelievable. Now, when I do a board meeting or something like that, it's like a day in the country.

To make it as a caterer, you have to be honest with yourself and ask yourself how creative you are and how much you value creativity. For me, it's the big kahuna. If I don't feel I can be creative, then I feel stifled. That's why I love social catering. I come up with a million different ideas for weddings and bar mitzvahs and I love it. My girlfriend, who started with me, is more of a straight meat-and-potatoes type—or should I say chicken salad-and-cold cuts—and so she's gone into corporate catering, where you don't have to reinvent the wheel every time in order to have a satisfied customer.

I've known people who fled social catering for corporate catering, thinking that they would find great oases of sanity in that world. But corporate catering comes with its own set of problems. For one thing, you're often dealing with major crowd scenes, so you really have to know how to figure your portions and your costs. On the other hand, I find that corporate clients are less apt to dicker with the price. They just want to make a good impression, and until recently, when the economy swan dived, they had money to spend.

If you're on the fence between social catering and corporate catering, you might want to get into the area of cultural catering, which is basically putting on events for museums, orchestras, ballet companies, charities, and so forth. There you're really going for image, as in the corporate world, but you've got more creativity, obviously, than in the corporate world. Then again, you don't have the money that you've got in the corporate world. Hey—life is all about trade-offs, right?

The Making of a Great Caterer

Once you've established which area of catering interests you, next you must figure out whether you've got the stuff to become a really good caterer. What exactly is that "stuff"? Your fellow professionals comment.

- You have to be a four-star general—nothing less. This is not about serving somebody meat loaf and mashed potatoes, the way it would be if they came into your restaurant. This is about coordinating very, very big events, either in the life of an individual, a corporation, or a not-for-profit institution. That means that everything has to be just right: food, lights, music, parking, staff, the ice swan, the orchids, whatever. Wait a minute—you don't have to be a four-star general. You have to be a producer. You have to be a Cameron Mackintosh, and think of each event as the opening night of *Les Miserables!*

- It helps to have something of a good math head. I don't mean you have to be an Einstein, but you are dealing with figures. You have to understand quantities and prices and ratios and all that. If you're totally math phobic, either deal with it, or hook up with someone who isn't.

- To make it as a caterer, you need to have a service orientation. In a sense, all aspects of being a culinary professional are service sector, but if you're a chef in the kitchen, you don't have to be eyeballing your customer.

As a caterer, however, you are going to get into a lot of face-to-face, and liking people, or at least being open to people, is critical. When I cater a party, I take it as seriously on an emotional level as the hosts do. That's why I'm a great caterer.

꙳ Stamina helps. Like everything having to do with cooking, you're on your feet a lot. Get a good pair of shoes.

꙳ Grace under pressure, my friends. You're going to be dealing with crises all the time. The florist is going to deliver pink carnations instead of white daisies. The wine order's going to be a case short. You're the one that's going to be dealing with all of this. Screaming and temper tantrums are not the answer.

Specialty Caterers

You may find it extremely helpful when launching a catering business to have a recognizable niche. Your fellow professionals have this to say.

꙳ I started out as an all-purpose, mainstream, social caterer. Then I switched to kosher catering. Of course, being Jewish helps, but I found that it cut the competition in half. There were other kosher caterers in town I was competing with, but coming up against a couple of kosher caterers is a whole lot better than coming up against a couple of dozen all-purpose caterers.

꙳ My catering business took off when I went totally organic and vegetarian. For one thing, it sparked my interest a lot more, and I got a lot more creative. For another thing, it was a good "hook" for an event. Since

I mostly do cultural catering, I'm dealing with a very educated, sophisticated clientele, and they've been thrilled to get behind me when I put on an organic function.

🌡 I only do seafood. Everybody loves seafood, but not everyone does it well. Not only do I have access to the best fish suppliers in the city, but I can pull together a raw bar, a sushi bar, fish and chips, clambakes, and I've partnered up with a guy who has a pleasure yacht for certain events. Of course, I smell like fish most of the time, which doesn't help my love life any, but what are you going to do?

🌡 I've made a name for myself by becoming the "picnic lady." I do incredible box lunches—just like mama used to make. Really delicious fried chicken and potato salad and super fudgy brownies. I can do bento boxes if people want. I get a lot of business from schools and colleges—places that have lots of nice green space where you can enjoy al fresco meals.

The How-To of Catering

While you're not going to get a comprehensive education here in how to run a catering business, some top tips follow from professional caterers:

🌡 You could be the greatest cook in the world and know exactly where to find the prettiest centerpieces, and your business can still go belly-up in a flash *if you don't run it as a business!* That means before you even get your business cards printed up, you have to figure out a few crucial things about setting up your systems. You have to know how to price. You have to know how to market. And you have to have all your insurance and necessary permits in place.

🌿 Pricing is tough, but pricing is ultimately what will make or break your business. And you don't want to figure it out on the cuff, or go back to a client after the fact and say, "Golly gee, I didn't charge enough for that shrimp scampi. Would you mind giving me another 50 bucks?"

🌿 A lot of factors go into your pricing. You've got your raw materials, your labor, your client's budget, the complexity of the job, if there is any rush element to the job, if you're competing against the bids of other caterers, and so on. As a rule of thumb, though, you can begin your estimate with your ingredients, your time, and your overhead.

🌿 Let's get this out of the way right away: you're going to underprice in the beginning. Everyone does. It's going to take you longer to get things done, which is one reason why you're not going to be adequately compensated for your time, and then the experience issue comes into play, because in the beginning, you're not going to be experienced in the fine art of giving estimates. In time, it'll work out, though.

🌿 To really get the hang of giving estimates, you have to be out there networking with other caterers. Don't just think of other caterers as your competition.

Nobody can do it all, and so there are some functions that you'll have to miss and others that your friendly caterers in the neighborhood will have to forgo. So if you see each other as a support network instead of sharks in a tank, you can help each other. And one way to help each other is to put your heads together on prices and figure out the going rate.

✑ Costing on food is a laborious process. It involves keeping careful notes of your buying patterns and recording the best prices you get on the various items.

✑ I was taught that the way to figure is to take the cost of your ingredients for a meal and to multiply by three to get the final overall cost. This is just to make back your ingredients, labor, and overhead. Anything else—music, decorations, flowers, liquor—is computed separately. Then you divide the figure you come to by the number of servings, and you get your per-head cost.

✑ What constitutes a fair profit margin in this business? The way I figure it is a gross profit of 30 to 40 percent [that] leaves me with a net profit of 10 to 20 percent. If business is steady, I can get by on 10 percent, but I'm not going to be buying myself a new Lexus every year, thank-you very much.

✑ In terms of figuring in your labor costs, look at your menu. If you've got a labor-intensive menu, you have to divide your factored cost by the number of labor hours you're projecting. If you've got a menu that's pretty easy to prepare, you can raise your price a little and make a better profit.

Working with Staff

How about some good tips to help you make the most of the people you bring into your business?

✐ Figure out what you absolutely have to do yourself. You don't delegate seasoning, for instance. You might get someone who has no idea how to use dried chilies, and he sets the whole place on fire.

✐ I like to rotate tasks so that no one gets stuck with just peeling potatoes. That seems to go a long way toward keeping people happy.

✐ Make sure your kitchen is well set up, with as many definable stations as you can create.

✐ Be a teacher and be a student. Show your staff how you like things done, but also be open to learning new ways of doing things.

✐ Make sure you give people breaks. It recharges them, and they work better.

✐ *Be nice.* Don't snap at people or take out your tension on them. It's not good for them, and it's not good for you.

Menu Planning

There's so much to think about in the menu planning area. Some tips we felt we had to share from professionals follow:

✐ I like to have at least one—and in many cases no more than one—showstopper for every meal. It's the thing that will get people to remember me. I don't know what it is—that will depend on the client—but we're talking about things like the proverbial Baked Alaska (or a more contemporary twist on it) where you've got the oohing and aahing going.

✍ As in any menu, a chief concern is balance. Do you have nice crispy greens to go along with creamy mousse-y things? Sweet and savory? Yin and yang? That's what makes a good menu.

✍ Obviously, there's a great benefit to any foods that you can prepare ahead of time. And there are many foods that actually improve with a little age, like ragouts and stews and such, so keep that in mind.

✍ You always have to think of costs when you're preparing menus, and not just the cost of ingredients. An expensive ingredient might lift a simple dish off the ground, and you're saving on labor costs. A cheap dish that has 50 steps won't save you any money in the long run.

✍ Use in-season foods. People love fresh tomatoes and summer corn and all that. And your ingredients will be far cheaper that way. Tracking down asparagus in the middle of the winter is not a way to go. On the other hand, an off-season item that's used as a glamorous garnish—like fresh raspberries out of season—can be an effective touch.

✍ Dressing up inexpensive, ordinary food items is a good trick. The time-honored radish rose is a case in point.

You have to gauge your menu to the event. What kind of foods do people really like to eat at cocktail parties? (Obviously they're not going to sit down with a polenta, right?) How interested in food will they be? People really do eat at weddings, for instance, because it's a long event. People at buffets eat less than people at sit-down dinners. You'll get to know all these things in time.

Shopping Tips for Caterers

More ways to save money and time follow:

Stock up on specials that can be frozen, such as meats and poultry. Just make sure you're scrupulous about marking dates on whatever you freeze away.

Certain items must be purchased on the day of the event. Day-old bread is not appropriate at a catered affair, and you want your fish and salad greens to be as fresh as possible.

Never fudge! Never slip a box of cookies for your child into your client's food bill. It's highly unethical, and you'll live to regret it.

If you're dealing with food wholesalers, which can be very advantageous, make sure you get a guaranteed delivery time, and be prepared to pay cash upon delivery. Make sure that they understand that you only want the best, and that there will be no second chances. Check your items upon delivery to make sure they're just as you want them.

As we said at the top of this chapter, the amount of space we have to talk about the different opportunities in the "range of opportunities" is limited. We will have to leave the field of catering without discussing many important issues, such as stocking a bar and assessing your kitchen facilities. You will need to do a great deal of thinking and research if you plan to go into catering. This has just been a "taste." Now let's move to another field: personal chefs.

Getting Personal

A growing and an exciting area for culinary professionals to explore is becoming a personal chef. Why? Let's hear from your colleagues.

✐ I did it for the money. I was working at a top, top restaurant in Chicago, and I was grossing eight dollars an hour right out of cooking school. After a while, it went up to 11 dollars and change. I was pulling out my hair trying to make ends meet. Of course, I was getting a great apprenticeship, but then I felt like, "Okay, show me the money . . . or at least *some* money." Then a friend of mine put me in touch with an agency that specializes in hiring private chefs, and in a minute I had a job working for the CEO of a Fortune 500 company. I was making twice my salary for fewer hours, plus I had health insurance. Of course, I couldn't have done it without putting in the apprenticeship in the restaurant, but this is a direction that more people should know about.

A good private chef can make between $50,000 and $100,000 a year.

✍ I *love* my job as a personal chef. I work for an internationally known sports figure who also happens to be a compete doll. He's really fun to cook for, because he's a very adventurous eater. He goes all over the world and comes back on a kick for Jamaican food or Thai food or whatever, and I have to keep up. It's a great challenge.

✍ I enjoy my job because not only do I have a lot of creative freedom, but also there are no budgetary constraints to speak of *and* I'm a salaried employee. That means if my boss takes off for a week to Singapore and I stay home, I'm cooking for myself and getting paid for it.

✍ For a lot of us, the job of personal chef is a kind of fantasy. We think of Rosie cooking for Oprah and it's like, "Where do I sign up?" But believe me, like everything else in life, there is a definite down side. I work for a Hollywood mini-mogul, and he's such a narcissistic baby. Which is bad enough, but food pushes people's emotional buttons, and sometimes he thinks I'm mama. He'll call me at midnight and ask me to make him potato pancakes. That's when I want to kill him.

✍ To be honest, the boundaries around being a personal chef can get a little fuzzy. Sometimes they think you're the maid or an *au pair* or something, and they'll ask you to walk the dog or pick up the kids somewhere. That's when you either pull out the job description or, more likely, start looking for another gig.

✎ You have to be able to choke down stuff if you're working as a personal chef. I realize this is going to sound strange, but the very, very rich are not like you or me. They can get weird. I know personal chefs who've had to make ridiculously lavish tea parties for four-year-olds or brunch for the pet pug. It's possible for you to reach a point where you just have to say, "Enough. I'm out of here. While I can still hold on to my values."

✎ I've worked for some spoiled brats. I was a chef on this guy's yacht for a while, and he and his insufferable girlfriend would actually send dishes back to the kitchen. I wanted to scream, "Have you seen the *size* of this kitchen, King Louis? I'm doing the best I can!"

✎ One thing you may not think of when you decide to become a personal chef is that not only will you be cooking the dinner but you will be serving the dinner and cleaning the kitchen. For the most part, we're not talking about some English country estate with 12 maids upstairs and 12 downstairs. This is you—just you—and a whole lot of work.

✎ You have to have real people skills to do well as a personal chef. "Personal" is the operative word here. And, most likely, you're going to have to audition for this job, so your pleasing, sunny personality has to be on display from the get-go.

✎ I like the job because it's a total learning curve. In the restaurant world, you learn by doing your rotations, if you're lucky, or staging—working for free in a kitchen for a day here or a day there. As a personal chef, you're doing a lot of self-directed learning. For instance, I made a point of educating myself about wine because my boss had an extensive wine cellar, and I needed to know about it. My chances of learning as much about wine in a regular restaurant kitchen wouldn't even come close.

 You know what's really good about being a personal chef? You're often meeting rich people. That's who comes to these dinners I make for my boss. And if I ever decide to open a restaurant, I'll have this pool of potential investors to check in with. Or, better yet, maybe some fabulously rich guest will fall in love with my *quenelles de brochet* and decide to marry me!

 Being a personal chef requires a whole other kind of tempo and tenor from working in a restaurant kitchen. You have to run out and buy things because they're not where you would expect them to be. You have to cook with four burners. You have only a small group of people to applaud your efforts. There's no real spotlight. You're not going to win any Chef of the Year awards. It takes some getting used to.

 As in any business, plan on supporting yourself for six months to a year while preparing to become a personal chef. It's a good idea to get training through a personal chef association, such as the United States Personal Chef Association <http://www.uspca.com>. This association can provide inexpensive liability insurance, certification through classes, and a self-help

Sanitation for Caterers and Personal Chefs

Sanitation and the proper storage of uncooked and cooked food is a must. Consider taking the ServSafe© course from the National Restaurant Association <http://www.nraef.org>. The certificate is helpful when approaching new clients.

course that covers setting up an office, licenses required, marketing, and answers to all your questions.

Demonstration Chefs

Another interesting area for culinary professionals to look into is the role of a demonstration chef. This position combines teaching with cooking. A demonstration chef works for cooking schools, in supermarkets, and, at the top of the heap, on television.

Teaching Cooking Classes

Teaching cooking classes is a wonderful way to get around in the food world, and it is highly recommended for anyone who aspires to write cookbooks and/or to go on television. Your fellow professionals comment.

✑ The usual gig runs about two to three hours and you should expect to create three to five dishes, which your students will consume. A successful class will be big on entertainment value—how well you communicate and how exciting your dishes are (nobody's going to get all worked up about a grilled cheese sandwich)—as well as on the educational value (can people replicate this at home?) and the dining value (does it taste good when they sit down to eat it?).

🍮 The going rate that I've heard of is anywhere between $300 and $1,000 per appearance. Your traveling expenses—hotel and transportation—are on top of that.

🍮 It's important that you get a firm commitment—that is, in writing—from the school spelling out a cancellation fee. I'd say 50 percent of your fee would be a fair cancellation policy.

🍮 Good communication is a must. You must never put the school in the position of running after you to have their questions answered and their anxieties allayed. Make sure you answer your e-mails, pay attention to your cell phone, and all that.

🍮 When you plan your lesson, consider the sophistication level of your audience. Of course, generalities can always be debunked, but as a rule, if you're doing a cooking lesson in some affluent urban/suburban neighborhood, like Marin County or Winnetka, you're more likely to score a hit with highly adventurous dishes than if you try them out in Terre Haute or Kankakee.

🍮 As in all fields in the culinary world, a high level of organizational skills is crucial. Everything needs to be laid out in advance, and if you are using assistants, you need to talk to them ahead of time to make sure that everyone's on the same page.

Television Chefs

Oh, to be another Emeril or Julia Child or one of the Two Fat Ladies. Seriously, in our media-crazed society, no pinnacle is more sought after for the culinary professional than a perch on the little screen. So what is the best way to go about realizing this dream? Your colleagues offer the following advice:

✧ It takes a lot of hard work to look easy and natural on television. And that's what TV success is all about—looking easy and natural. Do you remember the old *Honeymooners* episode when Ralph Kramden went on TV as the "Chef of the Future"? TV has the capacity for making you look entirely ridiculous. If you want to be a TV chef, start by watching TV chefs and studying every move they make.

✧ You need to develop a résumé, as well as real experience, so go after local TV, cable access, anyone who'll have you.

✧ Whenever you appear on TV, always get a tape. The producers will be happy to give you one.

✧ Bring a lot of food with you, and feed people a lot—the hosts, the technicians, the audience, whoever. Food makes people happy, and the more you manage to make people happy, the more likely you are to be asked back.

✧ Always smile. Constantly smile. For no reason. You may think you'll come out looking like a jack o'lantern, but, believe me, smiling looks great on TV.

✒ You realize, of course, that to be a successful culinary professional, you have to be organized in the kitchen. *Mise en place* and all that. Well, for TV, you have to take that rule and multiply it 20 times. You have to be an unbelievable Swiss watch to make it on TV. All of your ingredients have to be lined up in chronological order so that you don't fall off the wagon. Check out the kitchen before you're on the air. Don't go to your shoot expecting a gas stove and then—surprise! —when you get to the studio you find out that it's electric.

✒ I always bring my very special items with me. You know the way some people travel with their own pillow? I travel with my own cutting board, my own ladle, and I used to travel with my own chef's knife before September 11, after which you couldn't get on a plane with a chef's knife anymore.

✒ Remember your posture. Don't hunch over. Hunching looks terrible on TV.

✒ If you're wearing an audio pack, learn how to turn it off. You don't want to be embarrassed having the audience hear what they're not supposed to hear.

✒ Having a niche helps. Something—anything—to make you stick out from the crowd.

✒ Try to communicate in memorable little sound bites. Don't even attempt to keep up a running commentary. Just the well-turned phrase here and there.

You want to be able to explain your recipe in a few well-chosen words. "I'm making a Filipino Adobe Chicken which I simmer first in a mix of soy sauce, water, bay leaves, and chipotle, and which I finish off on the grill." Nice, simple, and to the point.

✧ If you make a mistake—and you will—don't let it throw you. A little self-deprecating humor goes a long way. Nobody expects perfection because nobody—and I do mean nobody—is perfect. That's why Julia Child was such a hit, because she was so human and even eccentric.

✧ Convey a real love and passion for what you do. It'll make you glow on TV.

In this chapter we have touched on some of the more high-profile opportunities in the culinary field. There are others. You could work in food services for a college or a secondary school, at a spa, in test kitchens, or in a supermarket setting. We do not have the space to go into all of these positions, but you should know that they exist. Like looking at a wonderful menu, it can be hard to choose from such a variety of opportunities.

Thanksgiving Turkey

Certain foods are almost unavoidable in a chef's life. Whether you are working in a restaurant kitchen, are a caterer, or are a private chef, you will probably wind up serving turkey at Thanksgiving time. Roast turkey is a simple dish that is hard to make well. So often it comes out dry. The best way we have found to counter the dryness is to brine the turkey ahead of time, which will produce a succulent bird that will help you earn a reputation for excellence. The proportions that follow are geared for a 12-to-14 pound turkey. Remember, too, that the quality of the turkey, with free range being at one end of the scale and giveaway turkeys with pop-up thermometers at the other end, also will determine the quality of the finished dish.

- Bring two gallons of water to a boil in a large stockpot. Add 3/4 cup kosher salt and 3/4 cup sugar. Some cooks will add other flavorings to the brine as well, such as carrots, onions, celery, leeks, bay leaves, peppercorns, and thyme. These are optional, but interesting. You can experiment. Even without them, however, the basic brine of salt, sugar, and water will work wonders.
- Refrigerate brine until cold.
- Remove giblets and liver from the turkey, and reserve for other use, if desired. Add the turkey to the stockpot with the brine. If necessary, weight the turkey down with a plate so that it stays below the brine's surface. Refrigerate for 72 hours, then remove the bird from the brine and allow it to come to room temperature.
- Preheat oven to 425°. Loosely fill the turkey at both ends with stuffing, and truss it.
- Place the turkey in a large roasting pan, and roast until it starts to brown, around 25 minutes.

Reduce the oven temperature to 350°, and roast for 12 minutes more per pound. The turkey will be done when an instant-read thermometer inserted into the deepest part of the thigh reaches 165°. Baste frequently during the cooking with pan juices and olive oil or butter. If the turkey begins to darken too much, cover it loosely with foil.

- Remove the turkey from the oven, leave it covered, and allow it to rest for 20 minutes before carving.

This recipe will serve 15. Note that for safety reasons, the Health Department recommends that turkey be cooked unstuffed to eliminate the danger of stuffing that has not been cooked all the way through.

Chapter 12

The Savvy Professional

Y ou work long, hard hours in a field that is very demanding. The good news is that you have the potential to make a very fine living. You also have chosen a field where you will likely change positions with some frequency, so managing your career will become a critical part of your work as a culinary professional. You need to be flexible, forward thinking, and proactive. If a job no longer feels right—if the standards in the kitchen are not up to snuff; if your employers do not value you as you wish to be valued; if you feel you've come to a dead end; if you just need a change—then it's time to do something about it. Inertia is anathema to success.

The good news is that the job market is fantastic for culinary professionals. It is quite varied, and there is tremendous opportunity for upward mobility, as long as you possess two characteristics: attitude and attendance. In other words, you have to be able to show up for work each day—*on time*—and you have to show that you know what it means to be a team player. If you develop a reputation for those traits, and if you know your way around the kitchen, you should be in a good position when job seeking.

Laying the Groundwork

Before you start looking for a job—whether it's your first, second, third, or fourteenth—you should always do a self-check to assess your qualifications. Your colleagues comment.

✐ Sometimes people will come after you for a job, particularly in a field like the restaurant industry, where word of mouth is so strong. But in most cases, you'll be the one to kick off the process. Start by conducting a "review" of yourself. Don't wait to see how others in the field view you. First view yourself, and decide how you measure up.

✐ I "grade" myself every six months, whether I'm looking for a job or not. I do it as a matter of course. Okay, maybe that makes me sound like some kind of weirdo, but it works for me. Here's what I do: I keep a checklist of attributes, and every six months I go through my checklist, and I give myself a letter grade, A through F. Was I punctual? (I'm running a B there.) Did I get along with people? (Another B.) How was my appearance? Was my uniform always clean? How are my skills progressing? Am I getting faster? More efficient?

〜 You need to have a good self-image before you head out into the job market. Going for a job, hat in hand, thinking that you're really not that well qualified probably has more to do with you and all the emotional baggage you're carrying around than with any kind of reality. Getting feedback from close friends and colleagues about your qualifications or even having a few sessions with a counselor to work on your self-image could be useful.

〜 You really have to know what *you* want before you head out into the job market. Are you looking for security? The fast track? Flexible hours? More or less responsibility? Where do you want to be in a year? Two years? Five years? Being clear about your passions and priorities is important.

〜 We all hear a lot about "dream jobs." Don't buy into it. Dream jobs are like dream families—does anyone you know have one? All jobs come with their problems, some worse than others. The problems are usually things like too much work, crazy people, long commutes, no room for advancement, or any and all of the above. It's up to you to figure out what you think you can live with.

Calling It Quits

There's a right way and a wrong way to leave a job. Your fellow culinary professionals offer this advice.

✍ First rule of advice, which I'm sure you've heard from your mother, your father, your aunt, and your uncle: don't leave a job until you *have* a job. Even if you're miserably unhappy, tough it out, because you run the risk of being even more unhappy if you wind up experiencing a significant period of unemployment.

✍ You may have to do some serious planning before you leave a job. For instance, there might be some area in which you need to brush up your skills. If you're a sap when it comes to sauces, you might want to take a month to learn about sauces—on somebody else's coin—before you go out into the marketplace.

✍ Even if you've had heated words with your employer or the head chef while you're on a job, it's a very good idea when you leave for your new position to put the very best face on it. Most people will welcome the chance for civility. If you're the one who has to be the bigger person, then just bite the bullet and do it.

✍ Never give less than two weeks' notice, no matter how bad things are. Your goal is to come across as a class act, no matter what, and bad habits, like leaving without sufficient notice, become part of your biography that will follow you around. By the same token, never give more than four weeks' notice.

More than that, even if the situation is basically amicable, can become quite strained and awkward.

🍤 If you tell your employer that you're leaving, and he makes you a counter-offer, give it some serious thought. What is your leaving really all about? If it's about money, does it make more sense for you to stay than to transition into a new position? If it's about change, do you think maybe it would be a good idea for you to stay in the job as long as some changes do occur?

🍤 The best way for a person to leave a job is in the middle of a lovefest. Send personal thank-you notes to all the people you've worked with. Buy them presents. Take people out to lunch. It's so much nicer that way.

 *Regarding Résumés*

A well-honed chef's knife is a cook's basic tool, and a well-honed résumé is the basic tool of a culinary professional in search of a job. The résumé, which is the written summary of your education and work experience, will tell potential employers, at a glance, all about your achievements. Some thoughts from your colleagues follow on the subject:

🍤 Rule #1: Keep it short and sweet. In a lot of fields, people are told that their résumés should not exceed one page in length. This is not as much of an issue in the culinary world, where it is very typical and not at all frowned upon to have held a fairly long string of jobs. Still, you need to keep it compact. Don't go off on tangents about how you studied yoga under some swami in Bhutan. It's not relevant, unless you're looking to cook in an ashram.

∽ The résumé should focus on the "meat and potatoes" of your accomplishments. How many meals do you turn out a week? What type of restaurants have you worked in? What kind (or kinds) of cuisine do you specialize in?

∽ In this industry, putting your G.P.A. from high school or college on your résumé doesn't really cut the mustard, as it were. The people who hire you don't really care if you were Phi Beta Kappa. They care whether you know how to bone a fish or carve a roast.

∽ As a culinary professional, you are surely aware of the importance of presentation. You don't just send a dish out naked into the world—you put a little garnish on the plate to make it as attractive as it can be. The same goes for your résumé. Make sure to put your résumé on good-quality paper. Don't go rainbow crazy. Maybe you think pink is your color, or that orange is cheerful, but other people might hate pink or orange, so why risk it? Stick with white, buff, or gray. To you it might be boring, but to other people it's classic. And hold the parsley garnish . . .

∽ You might have a great résumé in terms of layout and the accomplishments you're listing, but if you don't have the necessary contact information—address, phone number, e-mail address—then what good is it going to do? Make sure that your contact information appears on your cover letter as well.

✐ When it comes to résumés, there's a big argument over how to arrange them. Check with a librarian or on the Internet for format. Some people like to arrange the résumé by listing their positions chronologically, while others like to arrange it according to their accomplishments or abilities. You'll have to check it out and decide for yourself.

✐ Use simple language. Don't go overboard with all kinds of exaggerations. It just looks foolish.

✐ Don't forget to list any honors and awards you've received.

✐ Make sure your career goals pop out. If you're intent on working as a pastry chef, for instance, make that goal clear on your résumé.

✐ If cooking represents a career change for you, try to convey the transferable skills you're bringing with you to this new career. For instance, if you were a manager at a phone company in the past, pitch your managerial skills as part of your current package. After all, a big part of a chef's job is managing people.

✐ If you look at the literature on creating résumés, they'll stress how you should always use "action verbs." You *developed/achieved/created/coordinated/maintained/formulated/introduced* and so on. These words make you sound like a powerful force . . . which you may very well be. Don't just limit yourself to cooking. Present yourself as a fully-rounded team player. *I conceived a menu based on regional offerings* . . . that sort of thing.

❧ As a chef, you're probably quite good at fine details. You know how to follow a complicated recipe and get it right. Pay that same kind of attention to the details of your résumé. Misspellings and poor grammar can translate into points taken off. And in this competitive job market, you can't afford to lose points on stuff like that. Just ask a friend or family member to give your résumé the once-over. But make sure that person is a decent proofreader. (If necessary, go to a professional résumé service, and draw on their resources for this task.)

❧ Nothing, nothing, nothing goes into the résumé about salary requirements. Could that be any clearer? Any talk about salary is restricted to your interview, and only if and when the interviewer brings the subject up.

❧ No photos, please. They will only make your résumé look like the kind of "Most Wanted" notice you'd find in the post office.

❧ Don't bother including personal references on your résumé. It's safe to assume that everyone has someone who can speak well of him or her. Just list a few professional references. If a specific job asks for personal references on its job application, then that's another story.

❧ If nothing else, remember this rule: *Never, ever* lie on your résumé. It will only come back to haunt you, and when the grapevine gets hold of what you've done, you might have really serious problems finding a job in the town you live in.

Sample Résumé. The sample résumé that follows is well written. Of course, other kinds of formats also would be acceptable. Explore which one works best for you by consulting with a résumé-writing service, your school, or knowledgeable individuals, or by looking for more information in career books or on-line. (The information on the next page is from a real résumé but has been altered to protect the person's privacy.)

Cover Letters

Everybody talks about the résumé, but the cover letter is just as important. In fact, without a good cover letter, a prospective employer may never even get to your résumé. Some tips follow from your colleagues:

✺ The most important thing to keep in mind is that your contact information has to be on your cover letter. It's not enough just to have it on your résumé.

✺ If you're creative—as so many culinary professionals are—then the cover letter is the place to unleash a little creativity, not on your résumé. Develop an interesting first sentence. Reference a quote. Do what you will to capture the attention of the person who may be reading your letter. But don't go overboard. Don't do a rap poem, or draw a cartoon, or whatever.

✺ This may seem obvious, but you'd be surprised how many people just don't get it. *You never send a form letter for a job.* Every letter to every person must be completely customized.

✺ Your letter should be personal and appealing, but brief. Don't go into any special circumstances. Don't

Simon Meadows

42 Barclay Street   421-889-0287
Madison, New Hampshire 12098
simonm@hotmail.com

OBJECTIVE
Working Executive Chef

WORK EXPERIENCE

ROSEWELL FOOD SERVICES
Concord, New Hampshire
CONCORD RACE COURSE—CAROUSEL RESTAURANT
Sous Chef

- Responsible for *expediting production* of all food, and minute-by-minute *supervision* of the staff, for this *620-seat* restaurant. Responsible for food sales of nearly *1 million* dollars in six weeks. Requested to work special functions, such as the *Adams Gala Ball,* serving fine dining to 350 people. One of four professionals chosen to work with two *Master Chefs* on special functions. Responsible for *creating daily specials* and preparing food for banquets held daily at the restaurants. Responsible for working as expeditor and as a liaison between the front and back of the house. Gained a working knowledge of inventory and ordering procedures.

CAMERON'S ON THE LAKE
Harrington, New Hampshire
Line Cook

- Responsible for the *production* of all food for this *350-seat* American–Italian restaurant. Started as a cold preparation cook and advanced to running "the line." Gained experience of high production for à la carte service of up to 1,200 people per day. Gained experience *managing* several preparations cooks and up to eight line cooks. Responsible for preparation of *banquets of up to 250* people while continuing normal restaurant service.

FREEDOMVILLE REFRIGERATED LINES, LTD.
Freedomville, New Hampshire
Operations/Dispatch

- Responsible for *complete logistics* of groceries for the entire Northeast for the *1.5 million* square feet Distribution Center, including routing, tracking of shipments, and developing detailed reports for management. Fleet included over 200 owner-operators averaging 130 shipments per day.

Twelve years of front-of-the-house experience—Bartending in lounge, nightclub, wedding and banquet venues.

EDUCATION

WASHINGTON COUNTY COMMUNITY COLLEGE
Washington, NH, Associate in Occupational Studies—Culinary Arts

- Completion date scheduled for May 2003
- ServSafe©Sanitation Certification 12/12/01 * TIPS (Training for Intervention Procedures), Certified March 20, 2002.
- Recipient of the 2002 Lodge's Cooks Scholarship and the Marion Williams Scholarship
- Member of the American Culinary Federation (ACF)
- Member of Phi Theta Kappa—Alpha Upsilon Chapter

tell them how you had to sell the family farm in order to go to culinary school. Once you get your foot in the door—no, make that *beyond* the door—then you can get a little more personal.

🍮 Highlight your skills in your cover letter. If you've gotten special training in pastry or have done an internship with some well-known cook, let that be known right in the cover letter. It's a way to grab attention.

Networking

Far and away, networking is the culinary professional's best way to line up a job. In the food world, as in most industries, the worst jobs are those that are advertised in the "help wanted" sections of newspapers. In fact, the U.S. Department of Labor reports that only about 5 percent of job seekers will obtain their jobs through the "open" job market, which consists primarily of help-wanted ads on the Internet or in print publications. The food world is even more of a word-of-mouth industry than most, so networking is key. With your résumé in good shape, you can start to target those people you think might be of help. Keep in mind, however, the following pointers from your colleagues:

🍮 There's such a turnover in the food world that your best bet really is networking. I'm a chef and I teach culinary arts at a community college, and I probably get at least three to five calls a week from people who are looking to fill openings on their staffs. Some of the jobs are entry level; some are executive chefs. If I know people who are looking for jobs, I'm happy to make the connections. That's the way it's played in this business.

✑ You want to know why networking works? Because it's based on real human nature. People aren't helping you because of the goodness of their hearts. People are helping you because they figure that, down the line, maybe you'll help them or their sons or daughters or nieces or nephews. And if you're smart, you will.

✑ Try volunteering with different chefs so you can get your name out there in the community of culinary professionals. If you check into it, you'll probably find that there are fund-raisers scheduled in your area where chefs prepare food for hundreds of guests. Good help is always needed [at] these functions, and so this is a great way to get your foot in the door and make yourself noticed by a chef. If people see that you've got the right attitude and know how to be a team player, they'll be happy to help you.

✑ You never stop networking. It's a mind-set. It's not like you reach a certain plateau in your career and you just stop. You have to think of it as an ongoing activity that is positive and constructive for you and for the people in the field you respect, admire, and want to encourage.

✑ Once you start getting into a networking mode, even if you're relatively new to the food world, you'll start to see how many connections you can make already. There are friends, family members, faculty you've known, and all of their contacts, neighbors, merchants at stores where you shop regularly, people in your church or synagogue, or other organizations in which you participate. Start keeping track of them, developing a Rolodex or a database, and you'll be surprised.

✐ Always keep an up-to-date business card at the ready, and carry it with you at all times. There is plenty of software on the market to help you make your own, or you can have a few hundred run off inexpensively at any of the big copy centers.

✐ Keep in mind that networking doesn't just happen at business functions. The whole point of networking is that there are all kinds of people out there who can help you. So if your cousin invites you to join her at her law firm's Christmas party, take your business card with you. Maybe you'll wind up talking to a partner whose spouse owns a restaurant. You never know . . .

✐ When you exchange cards with someone, take a second to jot down some bit of relevant information about that person on the back of his or her card. Maybe the person was into sailing, as you are, or was an old movie buff. That kind of information will make for useful "openers" when you try to reconnect.

✐ Don't take it personally if someone doesn't seem interested in networking with you. It happens. Just move on.

꩜ If someone helps you in the course of networking—whether it's an actual job lead or just some good information—show your appreciation. Drop the person an e-mail to say thanks. It makes a difference.

꩜ Don't abuse these connections. If a person is open to networking with you, don't suddenly act like the two of you are the best of friends. That will turn off the other person very quickly.

꩜ Next to public speaking, networking is the big fear for a lot of people. Mingling with strangers at cocktail parties used to be my idea of hell on earth. The way I got around it was by practicing with people outside of my work world. So I'd give myself an assignment. I'd go to my kids' Little League games, and I'd tell myself to strike up a conversation on the bleachers with someone I didn't know. Then I'd find other places where I could practice my skills. The more I did it, the better I got at it.

꩜ Learning to mingle is a skill that, like any other skill, only gets better with practice. Don't get stuck with just one person at a networking event. That's not what it's for. Be friendly, and introduce yourself to as many people as you can.

꩜ Help others as much as you can. I'm of the belief that when you help other people, your good deeds come back to help you.

꩜ If you want to get a job, you've got to go after it. It's not going to come after you. I knew I wanted to work in food services at Disney World. It was just a dream I'd set for myself. So I went after anyone who was even close to Disney World. It took persistence, ingenuity, a tough hide, but within a year, I had my job. Of course, I had the qualifications too, which didn't hurt.

✐ If you're still in school, take advantage of the guest speakers who come to lecture. Target them—but nicely, please—after their presentation, and ask them if you could send them your résumé. Many will be open to such a proposition.

✐ I recommend that all job seekers join their local chapter of the American Culinary Federation <http://www.amchefs.org> and get involved. Once you join the ACF, they have a job posting site that members can log onto. There you can post your résumé and can check out the job listings that employers have posted.

Certification

More and more employers are looking for certification from the American Culinary Federation (ACF). The purpose of the certification is to ensure a nationwide standard for culinary skill proficiency. The highest levels of certification are the Certified Master Chef (CMC) and Master Pastry Chef (CMPC), both of which require days of rigorous testing. For more information, consult the ACF Web site at <http://www.amchefs.org>.

The All-Important Interview

The résumé and networking are designed to get your foot in the door. Now that you've done so, what's your next step? Your fellow culinary professionals comment.

✍ When a person applies for a *sous chef* or chef's job, he or she may be asked to prepare a meal for the managers or owners. When I got my job, I had to prepare a meal for eight, plus do a cold plate for a buffet.

✍ Before I got my job, I had to work a couple of shifts in the kitchen. That's not unusual.

✍ When you go for your interview, make sure, first and foremost, that you have identification with you. That means a Social Security number, a driver's license, the names and addresses of former employers, and the name and phone number of the nearest relative not living with you. Don't leave home without these!

✍ First impressions count for a lot. That's just the way the world works. Think of how you've felt on occasions when a blind date comes to your door. Well, when you go into an interview, you're the blind date. That means your grooming and your uniform have to be spotless. Leave your gravy stains at home, please!

✍ A lot of people these days *hate* perfume, and probably nobody hates perfume more than people in the culinary field, who rightly believe that it interferes with smell and, ultimately, with taste. So forget about wearing perfume for your interview. In fact, kick the perfume habit altogether.

✎ Bring an extra copy of your résumé with you to the interview. Even though you may have sent one beforehand, it can't hurt to have another one with you.

✎ Smile. People like smiling faces.

✎ There's no being late for interviews . . . *ever!* You should figure that if you're just one minute late, or even 30 seconds, you've lost that job. Scout out the location of your interview a day in advance. Even if it's an hour away, make the run. It's worthwhile, because if you get lost on the day of your interview, even if you show up officially on time, you may still wind up looking all hassled and stressed, and that won't help anything.

✎ Whatever you do, do not criticize a former employer. It will only reflect poorly on you.

✎ Anticipate questions. Obviously you know that certain ones are going to be coming up. *Why do you want to work here? What do you think you could contribute to our operation? What's your best dish?* You need to do your homework, and make sure that you've got some good responses handy.

✎ I tell the cooks I mentor to compile as many possible interview questions as they think they might encounter. Are you a team player? Are you flexible? What are your career goals? Are there any obstacles that would keep you from fulfilling your commitments? What chefs have influenced you most? Any and all of these may come up, so it helps to be ready.

✐ Role-playing your interview with friends or family can be very useful. Just make sure you're doing it with someone who knows how to take the charade seriously.

✐ Hey, people—don't use the interview as a time to have a coffee break, okay? You don't walk in with a cup of java or a can of Coke™ or some Ritz™ crackers . . . even if this is the food world. You don't chew gum on an interview. And smoking? Are we kidding?

✐ Sit up straight, and speak clearly, just like your mother told you to.

✐ There will come a critical point in the interview when the interviewer will sit back and say, "Now do you have any questions for me?" This is not a time to sit there, looking pretty and shaking your head no. This is a time for you to seem like an intelligent, engaged person. So come prepared with a few questions. Not a whole barrage of them—just a few well-chosen ones.

✐ Don't forget to follow up your interview with a thank-you note. It's required. And it will give you the opportunity to restate your eagerness to fill the position, which could wind up being a key factor if the interviewer is choosing between two or three people.

✐ Keep in mind that there are certain questions that an interviewer does not have the right to ask, and that you do not have to answer. Anything having to do with your race, religion, national origin or citizenship, age, marital status, sexual preference, disabilities, physical traits . . . these are all strictly off-limits. If one of these questions comes up, you should politely but firmly state that you do not think the question is relevant to the position being filled, and that you would like to focus on those qualities and attributes that are relevant. The message should sink in, and your interviewer may actually wind up being impressed with your presence of mind.

Stagiares

An interesting experience to be had in the culinary field is what is known as a *stagiare*, or an apprenticeship, in a chosen restaurant. Think of a stagiare as one part educational experience, one part networking and one part interview. The stagiare can be for a one day-one shift event or for a longer period of time. In New York City, it is quite common for cooks to participate in stagiares in many restaurants. This way they can pick up new techniques after their regular shift at the restaurant in which they are working. Participating in stagiares is how the really great chefs pick up their skills, and "staging" is something you can do at any point in your career. It may take a lot of perseverance to set up a stagiare, but it can be so well worth it.

Salary Negotiations

For some people, talking about money is like a trip to the dentist: they'll do anything to avoid it. But it doesn't have to be that way. Talking about money is a completely natural part of the hiring process, and you need to become comfortable with the idea so you will be able to better negotiate your salary. Some tips follow from your colleagues regarding this negotiation.

✑ Do your homework. Know what the going rate is in the neighborhood for the position being filled. The more information you have, the more powerful your negotiating position will be.

✑ Negotiating for a job is not like negotiating for a car. After you buy the car, you'll probably never see the seller again. But with job negotiations, if the hiring goes through, you'll be living with the person you've been negotiating with, so it's important to operate out of goodwill. Keep in mind that if you're being offered the position, that means that the employer you're negotiating with has made up his mind that you're the one for the job, and so you both have the same goal: to make this happen.

✑ There are a lot of "extras" that factor into a total compensation package, and you need to be aware of what they are. It could be vacation time, health insurance, or whatever. Look into all of these, and weigh them carefully when you're making your deal.

꩜ Never lie. If you've got a job history already, never say you made more on your last job than you actually did. On the other hand, you don't have to show all your cards. In a way, salary negotiations are a little like a game of poker . . . a bit of bluffing may come into play. Maybe your first time doing it, it won't go as well as you hoped. But with practice, you may wind up winning a few hands.

꩜ Bargaining is expected, but there comes a time when you run the risk of overkill. When you feel the offer is in the zone, then back off. Don't hold out for every last penny. Even if your demands are met, your employer may walk away from the experience feeling that he has hired a prima donna. Remember that negotiation is about give-and-take all around.

The culinary field is full of exciting possibilities at every level. Keep your eyes and ears open, be proactive about your career, continually educate yourself to develop more expertise and familiarity with the cuisines of the world, and go for it!

Really Good Coffee and Really Great Tea

It is the American habit to end a meal with coffee, and nothing can make or break the reputation of a kitchen more quickly. A bad cup lingers in the mind; a good cup lingers on the palate. So why risk raising the wrath of your coffee-loving customers by serving anything less than really good brew? Some pointers follow:

- Process is one thing; the ingredients are another. And, when it comes to coffee, the ingredients are key. Always start with freshly roasted, whole-bean coffee. Coffee starts to decay once it has been roasted, and the decay accelerates once it has been ground. So if possible, always grind your whole beans right before you use them.

- The quality of the water you use can significantly impact on the quality of the coffee you brew. Does your town have "funny-tasting" water? If so, you will need to use bottled or filtered water.

- Make sure that you have the correct grind for your brewing process. Our very favorite method is to use a French press, and in that instance, the coffee should not be ground too finely. Discuss the brewing method you use with your coffee purveyor to get the grind you need. (Never use a percolator—it boils the coffee.)

- Be scrupulous about keeping your brewing equipment clean. Coffee oils that build up in the brewer can turn rancid and will produce an "off" taste.

- Some diners enjoy flavored coffees, while many loathe them. In fact, even the smell of some flavored coffees, such as hazelnut, seems to have the capacity to literally turn the stomachs of certain diners. Do everyone a favor and keep

separate grinding and brewing equipment for flavored coffees.

- A freezer is a good place to store whole coffee
  beans. They will keep up to a month there.

As for tea, the American habit of using tea bags is considered barbarous by tea drinkers in other parts of the
world. Make a proper cup of tea the following way:

- Follow the correct proportions of tea to water.
  One teaspoon of loose tea makes a six-ounce cup.

- Rinse the teapot with hot water to warm it. Do
  not use a metal teapot as it creates an off flavor.
  Use a teapot made of china, glass, or pottery.

- Bring fresh, cold water to a boil (see the coffee
  section regarding water).

- Place the loose tea in the pot, and pour the boiling water over it.

- Let the tea steep three to five minutes. Pour the
  tea through a strainer.

- Tea cannot be "held." It loses its freshness quickly. Make a new pot for each diner.

Chapter 13

The Possible Dream

Many wonderful paths can be chosen by the culinary professional, and we have discussed a number of them. Becoming a chef or a *sous chef* is just one path. Catering can be a terrific challenge and a great opportunity for the creative culinary professional. The position of pastry chef allows you to become deft at making all sorts of sweet things that bring people happiness. If you are a demonstration chef, you can work for cooking schools, in stores, or even on television (perfect for the culinary professional who also happens to be a great communicator). But one dream rises above all of the others in the food world, and that is to be a chef-owner.

Ideally, the chef-owner has a restaurant where a personal vision has become a reality. We think of famous chef-owners—Henri Soule of Le Pavillon, André Soltner of Lutèce, Wolfgang Puck of Spago, Alice Waters of Chez Panisse, Jasper White of Jasper's, Daniel Boulud of Restaurant Daniel, Anne Rosenzweig of Arcadia, Jeremiah Tower of Stars—and we aspire to that which they have experienced. These men and women have enjoyed total autonomy and great creative freedom. They have realized their dreams, and in so doing, they have made inestimable contributions to the culture of food. Could you possibly do the same?

In this chapter, you will hear stories and receive advice from chef-owners. These stories will inspire you, intimidate you, amuse you, and, hopefully, educate you. Even if you're not ready to move in that direction—even if you'll *never* be ready—you will no doubt find it interesting to hear what they have to say.

To Own or Not to Own— That Is the Question . . .

Owning or not owning is not a question to which we would even pretend to give a definitive answer, but it's interesting to hear the following people's thoughts on the topic:

✐ Owning a restaurant is so different from working in a restaurant. Suddenly, every night is like you're giving a dinner party. It's not just the food. It's the flowers. (*That florist slipped carnations in again!*) It's the glasses. (*Why are there streaks showing?*) It's the worrying about the spots on the carpet and whether there's toilet paper in the bathroom. Did I mention the staff? Did I mention the issues of advertising and marketing? Did I mention what it was like to get a bad review from a food critic who wouldn't know a good meal if it came up and bit him in the . . . leg?

✐ Some people say that owning a restaurant is like having people into your home for dinner six nights a week, and there's some truth to that. But that's what I *like* about it. I've made my restaurant feel like an intimate home—a heightened fantasy of what an intimate home is like. I mean, let's get real—your mother never cooked like I do. My mother never cooked like I do! But I've tried to get a real warmth and personal feeling into my restaurant, and people compare it to a home environment.

✐ The thing about owning a restaurant is that you're on 24/7. Even if you're not physically *there,* you're there. You're always thinking about it. I take a two-week vacation in the summer, when I close the place down, and believe me, it's not like any two-week vacation I used to have when I was working for somebody else.

✐ I just had to own my own restaurant. I mean, I was working in places that were considered good, but when I looked at some of the substandard food that they served, it killed me. Particularly for those prices. I just couldn't feel good about what I did. Now I'm struggling, although I think if I hold on long enough I'll be okay, but there's a real joy in knowing that you're serving people the best food. Not the most expensive ingredients or the most awe-inspiring presentations, but just really good, honest food.

❧ You wouldn't believe what my day is like. I get five hours of sleep if I'm lucky. I come in at three in the morning. Yeah—that wasn't a typo, folks. I'll set up my specials and write out my orders while the place is still quiet. Then, an hour later, my cook and dishwasher come in, and they start getting all the cleaning done. I take time to do some yoga, which is what keeps my head together. At 5 A.M., I'm placing the orders that I wrote out at 3 A.M. At 6 A.M, I start making my fancy cakes and tarts, which is one of the things we're known for (I started out as a pastry chef). At noon, I cook lunch. At two, I take a break and catch up with people on the phone. At three, I'm back to work, meeting with the staff, going over reservations, and so on. At 6, I'm cooking dinner. By 10, I'm out of there. Luckily, I live a two-block walk away.

❧ You have to do it all, but you can't do it all. What do I mean? I mean that you have to be good at all the important things—managing, dealing with people, finances, and cooking—but you can't micromanage. I can't do all of that plus peel potatoes. Something's got to give.

❧ The kitchen is the least of it, so if cooking is what drives your engine, you have to keep in mind that you might actually find yourself cooking less. More of your attention will be on the business of running the business and managing the staff. And chances are that stuff is going to be a learning curve for you. It sure was for me. In fact, I'm still working at it.

෴ Not having to deal ultimately with any authority but your own is worth everything. Every aggravation, every disappointment, every frustration—it all pales before the pure joy of being your own boss.

Jumping In

How do you know when the time is right for making the big jump and starting your own restaurant? Let's hear how other professionals decided.

෴ I have to say, and I'm not tooting my own horn, but I didn't have much of a choice. I found myself the hot new flavor in town all of a sudden, and I was young and photogenic, and people were running after me with money. It was like I was caught up in this riptide of fame, and I *had* to open a restaurant under my own name. Fortunately, I'm pretty well grounded, and I managed to keep a level head.

෴ I felt like I had no other choice. I had earned the restaurant I worked for four stars, and they weren't showing their appreciation adequately, as far as I was concerned. Translation: I was unable to separate them from more of their money. So I bit the bullet and headed out on my own. If I was as good as everyone said I was, didn't I deserve to make more money?

෴ I'd have to say that I rushed into it. I was so hot to trot to own my own place that I didn't give real thought to how much learning was involved. I mean, I'm not a businessperson, and you have to be. You can be the greatest cook in the world, but if you don't have a sense of a profit margin, then you're not going to make it.

✐ Starting a restaurant is a little like having a baby. It'll change your whole life. The amount of time and energy involved is phenomenal. It will affect your relationship with your spouse; it will radically cut into the amount of time you spend with your family and friends. Not that you can't make it work, but you just need to know what you're getting into.

✐ After a certain point, you need to make the leap . . . the leap of faith. If you tell yourself all the stuff you don't know—you don't know enough about pastry; you don't know enough about fish; you don't know enough about butchering—then you'll never do it. You don't need to know *everything* to start a restaurant.

The How-To of Starting a Restaurant

We wouldn't dream of trying to tell you all you need to know about starting a restaurant in the small amount of space we have here. As in other places in this book, we just want to give you a "taste." Sweet? Salty? Sour? Bitter? The experience of opening a restaurant can draw on all of these flavors. Your colleagues comment:

✐ I had a friend from culinary school who did something that I really thought was weird. He was a chef for a few years, and then, when he decided that he wanted to own his own restaurant, he took off a year to go work in another restaurant in the front of the house. He wanted to make sure he knew, firsthand, everything he needed to know about the table service, the bar, credit cards, the whole bit. Now that was dedicated, and that was smart. Most people wouldn't do that, but [he] was one of a kind.

◈ Settling on your location can be quite a process. I must have gone through 40 different "dream" locations before I settled on what I considered the right one. I was going to be in an office building. Then I was going to be near the big theater complex in town. Then I got real about the rents, and I started looking in residential districts, at brownstones, maybe with a little garden in the back. But the code issues were hell, and so I kept looking and thinking. I finally wound up at the port, because I love seafood, and I figured that would be a good theme. And it was. I lucked out. This big seaport restoration came in after me, and suddenly my cheap, offbeat location became prime.

◈ When you're picking out a location for your restaurant, you need to do what anybody who's looking for a store location would do. You sit in a parked car, like an FBI man, for days at a time, eating sandwiches, drinking coffee, and counting the passersby. If you don't count a lot, that means it's not worth the time, money, or effort to get started in that location.

◈ Restaurant design is a big issue. If you're lucky, you're a Wolfgang Puck, married to a top interior decorator like Barbara Lazaroff. Me, I'm lucky because I'm married to a wonderful woman, but she happens to be a nurse. So I started really small, with checkered tablecloths and hurricane lamps, but my food made up for it. Still, I dream about skylights and zinc bars and all that stuff. One day, maybe . . .

✐ I didn't have any real money for restaurant design, so I decided to have the whole focus be on an open kitchen. Well, that was the best decision I ever made. I even called my place "The Open Kitchen." People just sat there watching, like they were going to a show.

✐ You can cut back on a lot of things when you design your restaurant. You don't need original art on the walls or customized paint jobs or wall-to-wall mirrors. What you can't stint on is good lighting. Lighting that makes the food look good and the customer look good is what it's all about. I guess by now you've figured out that I mean no fluorescents, right? Nothing makes food—or people—look worse than fluorescent light.

✐ I called upon an old friend, who is an extremely talented graphic artist, to pull together my graphic look—my logo and my menu, my matchbooks, my cards, all that stuff. It's so important. I think it's just as important as your restaurant design. Those things are your advertising. You're not going to be doing TV spots. A matchbook is the way you're going to get your name around, and mine was just stunning.

✐ It's just like starting any business. You need a whole marketing plan. You need to get stories about you in the papers; radio spots; you need to go on local TV and do demos. The whole nine yards. If you're not up for that, you may have a problem.

✼ Figure out your targeted customers before you open your doors. Are you in an affluent urban or suburban neighborhood? Better have some classic dishes that are handled "litely." That's what's selling these days. Leave fat out of your main courses, and put it into the desserts. People seem to want to eat "litely" and then have "Death-by-Chocolate" afterwards. Ah, zeze Americains!

✼ What made my restaurant is that I became known for using a lot of local food growers, particularly those who raised crops organically. I wasn't strictly organic, but my interest in regional food growers struck a chord with the very liberal, educated clientele I was aiming for in my location. I'm in a college town, and people just really seemed to take to what I was trying to do.

✼ I found that a great place to make an impact is with your breadbasket. People are always dying to have good bread. They come in hungry, and it's the first thing they eat. And, when you come down to it, what's better than bread anyway, right? So for cheap and easy, you can make a big impression. I got into serving naan, the Indian breads, which are warm and puffy and perfect. People swoon and come to my restaurant just for the naan, I think.

✼ I introduced a cheese cart at my place. It's very special for most people to experience a cheese course after a meal, with really exquisite cheeses. It brings a whole other dimension to dining, and a whole other course you can charge for. It's been very popular and a great moneymaker. You've just got to take the time and make the effort to get educated about it if you're going to offer it.

✎ You better have great desserts. Most people in our society are crazed for desserts, especially when they go out to eat. You need a few real showstoppers in there. It's the last thing people eat, and it gets engraved on their memories.

Menu Planning

Here's a checklist for plotting out your menu (of course, you can change a menu at any time, and when you do, go back to this checklist).

✎ Is your menu set, or is it subject to change? Is the change seasonally driven?

✎ What are your signature dishes? Do you have a showstopper?

✎ Do you cook one basic cuisine, or do you borrow from many cuisines?

✎ How large is your menu? Do you have the staff to cover a large menu?

✎ What is the structure of your pricing? Do you offer items à la carte? Is yours a *prix fixe* system? Or is it *table d'hôte,* where you offer a single price for an

---

entrée that includes something with it, such as vegetables or a salad?

❧ How would you characterize the size of your portions?

❧ Do you have a wine list?

❧ Do you offer holiday meals?

❧ Which meal of the day is your menu geared toward?

❧ Is your menu descriptive, or do you rely on waitstaff to offer descriptions? If so, how are they trained for this?

❧ If you're opening a restaurant today, you've really got to invest, right from the start, in a good computer system. You'll be using computers to track inventory, make orders, handle reservations, do your spreadsheets. Your system will act as a database for recipes; it'll help you create menus; it will track salaries; do your bookkeeping. Too bad it can't clarify butter!

❧ Down the line, there's all kinds of amazing technology out there now that you can take advantage of when you start your own place. We're six years into our restaurant now, and all of our reservations are done through a computerized reservations system. We've installed an on-line reservation system that uses advanced handwritten character recognition, sort of like a Palm Pilot™. That gives you a very low, non-intrusive profile at the front desk, instead of one of those ugly big monitor things with a keyboard. The system gives you an instant "sketch" of any guest, so you know when they last dined with you, how many guests they brought with them, if it was a special occasion, and so forth. Guests can also reserve over the Internet, which is great.

✐ Not all technology has to be expensive to be terrific. We have all of our front-of-the-house team wearing vibrating pagers now, which allows the kitchen to communicate with them. One buzz means that the food is arriving at your station; two buzzes means that the food is arriving at your partner's station; three buzzes means you're wanted in the kitchen to answer a question.

Purchasing

One of the most important aspects of a chef-owner's work is purchasing. Effective purchasing impacts directly on the profit margin. You need to have an adequate storehouse of supplies so your restaurant doesn't get caught short. On the other hand, you certainly don't want to overbuy and throw away money. Some tips from professionals follow regarding purchasing:

✐ Create a master list (also known as purchase specifications or purchase specs) for foods, for equipment, and for any special service items. Review it often. If there are any changes in the menu, make sure that these changes are reflected in your master lists.

☞ Be as specific as you can in your master list. That means brand names, sizes, weights, federal grades, and so forth. You don't want any surprises in your inventory, unless someone is having a special, and you decide to veer from your list.

☞ Choose a purveyor for each item and a backup purveyor. People run out of things—that doesn't mean you should.

☞ How do you know if you're getting the best quality from your purveyor? Ask the important questions. Is the price quoted by the salesperson the same as the price on the receipt? Do you get the amount you asked for? Is the food in the proper containers? Are the invoices clear? Are the delivery trucks clean and refrigerated, if necessary?

☞ Here's my system. I do an inventory after each shift at each station—a quick once-over. Then I do my detailed inventories [in] weekly, monthly, quarterly, and yearly increments.

☞ Keep a purchase log. It eliminates guesswork as to what you paid for something and when and from whom you bought it. You may also have the unpleasant surprise, at some point, of being asked for point-of-purchase receipts by government agencies to determine the freshness of your shellfish or something like that.

The People Part

The food and the ambiance are obviously important aspects of a restaurant's success, but nothing will make or break your restaurant faster than service. Good service is memorable; bad service is unforgettable. You can be served an extremely delicious meal, but if you've been sitting in a restaurant virtually ignored for an hour, you won't even taste the deliciousness. And you will never come back. A critical part of a chef-owner's job is to manage people and to ensure the best level of service possible. Some tips follow on this subject from your colleagues:

✐ Bad managing results in lost time. There are never enough hours in our day, and every minute is precious. So I think of people as a resource, and if I'm not dealing with them effectively, I'm squandering that resource.

✐ Think "team." You're all in this together . . . or you should be. One way, obviously, to create a team spirit is to treat people fairly and to remunerate them fairly. Once you feel that you've been doing that, then you can focus on team-building activities, like sitting down all together to review the day and seeing how you can all maximize your time. The dishwasher, for instance, may be sitting around idle for a couple of hours. Couldn't he do a bit of prep work?

✐ Always take the time to carefully explain a task. That's called "training." If you don't take the time, everybody will wind up losing time. Show the person where the right tools for the job are kept. Discuss what to do in case of a failure or an emergency. Teach them how to assess their own performance.

꼬 It's crucial that you teach staff how to handle complaints promptly, courteously, and effectively. Not enough people get trained in handling complaints.

꼬 Learn to communicate. Use easy-to-understand, concise language. Encourage questions. Ask if people understand you, and make sure that the climate you've created allows them to say "no."

꼬 Make sure that your work areas are clean, well stocked, well ventilated, and safe. The relationship of worker to task is always determined, to some extent, by the environment, and nowhere is that more the case than in a restaurant kitchen. Have regular staff meetings to bring to light any problems in that area.

꼬 As the chef-owner, you're not only the big cheese, but you're the role model . . . or at least you should be. Don't smoke, don't drink on the job, and don't eat excessively. Make sure your appearance is as immaculate as you want your staff's to be. Be ethical and honest—always.

꼬 The more you relate personally to your staff, the more likely they are to relate to customers. And that's what it's all about. Nothing beats name recognition in terms of insuring customer return.

꼬 Service in our restaurant is our #1 priority. It has to be. We already know we're great cooks. We treat every one of our customers like a visiting dignitary. A waitperson is at the table within 30 seconds of the customer being seated. Entrées all come out at the same time. People feel pampered and loved, and they come back. No less than César Ritz said that "the customer is king." That was 80 years ago, and nothing has changed. The customer is still king.

✐ A restaurant is no place for snobbism. A restaurant is where people spend their own money—and sometimes quite a lot of money—and they should be able to get what they want. If that means they want to drink Coke™ with their squab, so be it. It doesn't appeal to me, but it's not my business.

✐ Some chefs will get very huffy about people coming in and going through a long list of dietary restrictions when they order. Some restaurants will even refuse to accommodate them, taking a "special orders *do* upset us" stance. In our restaurant, we look to accommodate people. We do no-salt, no-sugar, vegetarian dishes . . . whatever we have to do. After all, this is America in the twenty-first century. That's the way it is.

 *Promotion*

Another big concern for the chef-owner is getting her or his restaurant into the public eye and keeping it there. Let's hear how it's done by the following professionals:

✐ I do a special meal once a week. It might be an Indonesian *rijstaffel,* it might be something Russian in the middle of the winter, like borscht and buckwheat blinis, or I might do a *tapas* event. I e-mail the menu to a large list of people, and that way they have an awareness of me at least once a week, even if I go into the trash with all the other spam . . . you should excuse the expression.

🌀 Like so many other chefs, I do a lot of benefits and fund-raisers. It's a free way to get my name out there. I've been a mover and shaker with meals-on-wheels for years, and I do their big yearly event with a few other chefs.

🌀 I put together a newsletter several times a year. My wife and I both like to write, and we'll include reports of our trips to vineyards or other food sites, recipes, kitchen tips, and so forth. My customers seem to appreciate it.

🌀 Wine tastings are a boon. They really get people into your restaurant in an easy way.

🌀 Anyone who wants me on TV has got me. I don't care for what. If they ask, I show up.

🌀 Obviously if you can hire a good PR person to help you with promotion, all the better. A PR person can help you form a strategy for a whole year or more— not just opening night. They'll orchestrate the practice dinners and the opening party. They may be able to snare journalists, celebrities, concierges from the big hotels, food-world people—and all that matters.

Onward and Upward

Obviously there's a great deal more we could say about owning your own restaurant, but we're going to stop here. If you come to the place where you are seriously considering such a venture, you will have to spend months doing research, writing a business plan, becoming familiar with the statutes regarding workers' compensation and the laws regarding health regulations, educating yourself about taxes, and so on. As we said at the top of this chapter, we just give you a "taste" here.

This whole book, in fact, has been designed to give you just a taste of the many different aspects of what it means to be a culinary professional. Your profession demands continuing education if you are to evolve and become the very best you can be. As a great chef or as an owner, you should constantly be seeking out the best restaurants and the best food. Visit and dine at the restaurants that win national awards, such as the Nation's Restaurant News Hall of Fame, and observe what is done in these restaurants to make them unique. When you achieve what you have set out to do, you will likely enjoy material comforts, community respect, the ongoing joy of doing what you do well for a living, and camaraderie with your colleagues. You have chosen a great field—never forget that.

Index